GOD'S CALL

THE STOB LECTURES 1999

The annual Stob Lectures, normally devoted to the fields of ethics, apologetics, and philosophical theology, are presented each fall on the campus of Calvin College or Calvin Theological Seminary in honor of Henry J. Stob.

Dr. Stob, with degrees from Calvin College and Calvin Theological Seminary, Hartford Seminary, and the University of Göttingen, began his distinguished career as a professor of philosophy at Calvin College in 1939 and in 1952 was appointed to teach philosophical and moral theology at Calvin Theological Seminary, where he remained until retirement. He died in 1996, leaving many students influenced greatly by his teaching.

The Stob Lectures are funded by the Henry J. Stob Endowment and are administered by a committee including the presidents of Calvin College and Calvin Theological Seminary.

For more information on Dr. Stob and The Stob Lectures, see www.calvin.edu/stob.

GOD'S CALL

Moral Realism, God's Commands,
and Human Autonomy

JOHN E. HARE

WILLIAM B. EERDMANS PUBLISHING COMPANY
GRAND RAPIDS, MICHIGAN / CAMBRIDGE, U.K.

Wm. B. Eerdmans Publishing Co.
255 Jefferson Ave. S.E., Grand Rapids, Michigan 49503 /
P.O. Box 163, Cambridge CB3 9PU U.K.

Paperback edition 2001

Printed in the United States of America

06 05 04 03 02 01   7 6 5 4 3 2

Library of Congress Cataloging-in-Publication Data

Hare, J. E., 1949-
God's call: moral realism, God's commands, and human autonomy /
John E. Hare.
    p.   cm.
Includes bibliographical references.
ISBN 0-8028-4997-0 (alk. paper)
1. Christian ethics — Reformed authors.
2. Divine commands (Ethics) I. Title.

BJ1278.D58 H37 2001
241'.0442 — dc21

                                            00-063664

www.eerdmans.com

CONTENTS

INTRODUCTION

This book has three chapters, corresponding to three lectures which I gave at Calvin College in October 1999.[1] In this introduction, I will give an overview of all three, so as to give a sense of direction. I have called the book *God's Call: Moral Realism, God's Commands, and Human Autonomy,* and each part of the subtitle gives the content of one of the chapters. Taking the chapters together, what I am after is an account of God's authority in human morality. Here is an example of what I mean.

Peter has been married to Sue for many years, and he loves her very much. But she has a bad temper, and she has just let fly at him. This has happened before, and he has explained to her that because of an abusive environment while he was growing up, this kind of anger has a powerful destructive force over him. Now she has done it again, and he does not feel within himself the resources to get over it and be reconciled with her. He finds himself all used up. But he feels

1. I want to thank the Center for the Philosophy of Religion and the Erasmus Institute at the University of Notre Dame for funding which enabled me to pursue the research on which this book is based. I also want to thank the Calvin Center for Christian Scholarship, which enabled Robert Roberts and Linda Zagzebski to meet with me for a week discussing each other's manuscripts. The discussion was very fruitful, and the book has been substantially improved as a result.

none the less from outside himself the pull of the relationship towards reconciliation, and within that pull he hears the call of God. He judges that the relationship is still worth saving and that this is what God wants. In obedience to that call, but without joy, he starts to go through the steps again that will bring the two of them back together.

I think this kind of experience is familiar to believers in God and those on the edges of belief. In this book I am interested in three questions we might have about this sort of story. First, when Peter hears this call, what is the relationship between the inside and the outside? Is there really something outside him, calling him, or is this a colorful way of saying just that he is coming to realize what he himself most wants in the situation? I am going to defend a view I call 'prescriptive realism', which is the view that when a person judges that something is good, he is endorsing (from inside) an attraction (from outside) which he feels towards it. Second, even if there is some call from outside him, why bring God into this? There is the difficulty Plato pointed to in the *Euthyphro*. The pull of the relationship might be enough to explain Peter's sense of call, and the appeal to God might be redundant. Or it might be worse than redundant. It might tie the call to all sorts of ideas of divine reward and punishment which corrupt it. Third, what about Peter's autonomy? Doesn't this talk of God's call turn him into a child trying to please its father? Surely, as a moral agent he has the responsibility to decide for himself when he should stay with a relationship and when he should leave? These three questions are the topics of the three following chapters.

In the first chapter I will give a selective history of a sustained debate within Anglo-American philosophy over the last century between moral realists and moral expressivists. Moral realism is the view that moral properties such as moral goodness are real. Moral expressivism is the view that moral judgements are, to use a technical term, *orectic*. Greek has the term *orexis* to cover the whole family of emotion, desire, and will. Expressivism locates the role of moral judgment as expressing some act or disposition that belongs within this family. We can think of the debate as a disagreement about how objectivity and subjectivity are related in value judgment, and we will see different kinds of both objectivity and subjectivity in the course of the discussion. I think it is good at the beginning of a new century to look back at one's tradition and see where it has got to in the discussion of its central issues. I think this is a useful undertaking in itself. But theists have an extra reason in the present case, because the issue affects us closely. We feel pulled in two directions. We want to say that value is created by God and is there whether we recognize it or not. In that sense value is objective, and we feel pulled towards some form of realism. But we also want to say that when we value something, our hearts' fundamental commitments are involved. "Where your treasure is, there shall your heart be also," Jesus says in the Sermon on the Mount (Matthew 6:21). When we value something, spend time with it, sacrifice things for it, our deepest loyalty is expressed. In that sense our valuation is subjective, and we feel pulled towards some kind of expressivism. We have to have a way of saying both of these things together, and I am going to try to suggest a way.[2]

The second chapter will go back to the later Middle Ages, and in particular to the divine command theory of John Duns Scotus. I am interested in the relation he establishes between God's commands, human nature, and human will. I am going to try to show that a Calvinist version of the divine command theory of obligation can be defended via Scotus against natural law theory as well as contemporary

2. This is a project like that of Dooyeweerd, who has been influential at Calvin College where the lectures behind this book were originally given. Dooyeweerd wanted to say that there is for every modality a law side and a subject side, which is for human beings ultimately the heart or soul or spirit, the religious root or unity of human life. Dooyeweerd, however, was speaking from a different philosophical tradition, that of German idealism. I want to use the history of my own philosophical tradition to show how we can hold the objective and the subjective sides of evaluation together.

challenges, and I think it will be apparent how such a theory fits the account I am giving in the first chapter of the objective and subjective sides of evaluation. One theme will be that after the Fall our natural inclinations are disordered, and we cannot use them as an authoritative source of guidance for how we must and must not live.

Finally, in the third chapter I am going to go to the key juncture, as I see it, between the medieval discussion and our own times, and that is the moral theory of Immanuel Kant in the late eighteenth century. Kant has given us a central text which has been taken in modern moral philosophy to refute divine command theory. It is a text about human autonomy. I am going to try to show that Kant is not in fact arguing against the kind of divine command theory I want to support. I will discuss what Kant means by saying that we should recognize our duties as God's commands, and I will defend a notion of human autonomy as appropriation.

In each chapter I am trying to do philosophy through its history. This is a method which brings certain difficulties with it. It might seem easier just to do the history and describe what philosophers X, Y, and Z taught in the sequence in which they taught it; or just to do the philosophy and lay out a systematic account of the various topics in their interrelations. But just doing the history ends up being unfaithful to what makes this history important in the first place. And just doing the philosophy ends up making half-baked references to the history in which the topic is in fact embedded. Somehow we have to do both at the same time, and in a short book this has to be done briefly. The book is three moments plucked from a larger history and three thoughts abstracted from a larger framework. I hope the reader will nonetheless find them significant moments and important thoughts.

Chapter One

MORAL REALISM

In the first chapter I will present an account of the twentieth-century history of the debate within Anglo-American philosophy between moral realists and moral expressivists. Moral realists emphasize the reality of value properties such as moral goodness, a reality which is in some sense independent of our attempts at evaluation. I have used the term 'moral realism' because it is the usual term in this debate. But in this chapter my focus will usually be on values more broadly, and not moral values in particular. Moral expressivists emphasize the role of moral (or value) judgment in expressing the will or emotion or desire. Characterizing the two positions in this way reveals that they are not necessarily contradictory. Indeed, I will end with a kind of merger. But the merits of the merger can only be seen after looking at the history of the debate.

I have given a picture of the debate as I see it in the diagram on page 2. The diagram contains nine boxes, arranged with realists on the left and expressivists on the right. It construes the debate as a whole in terms of a structure in which both sides have made progressive concessions. That is why the nine boxes converge. I have put six concessions on the diagram, labeling them E for a concession by an expressivist and R for a concession by a realist, and numbering them chronologically. My own position is what I will call "prescriptive realism," which is a view that preserves, I claim, the surviving merits on

1

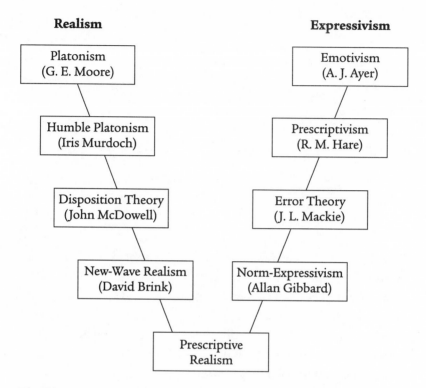

Realism

Platonism
(G. E. Moore)

Humble Platonism
(Iris Murdoch)

Disposition Theory
(John McDowell)

New-Wave Realism
(David Brink)

Expressivism

Emotivism
(A. J. Ayer)

Prescriptivism
(R. M. Hare)

Error Theory
(J. L. Mackie)

Norm-Expressivism
(Allan Gibbard)

Prescriptive
Realism

The Six Concessions

- R. M. Hare (prescriptivism — E1): Evaluative judgment is objective in a Kantian way.
- Iris Murdoch (humble platonism — R1): Humans are by nature selfish, and therefore our evaluative knowledge is precarious and incomplete.
- J. L. Mackie (error theory — E2): Evaluative judgment is by its meaning objective, in the sense that it claims to pick out features which are parts of the fabric of the world, and are there independently of us.
- John McDowell (disposition theory — R2): Values are like colors; they do not have to be seen as real independently of general human dispositions to respond to them in a certain way in appropriate circumstances.
- David Brink (new-wave realism — R3): An evaluative and a descriptive term that do not mean the same can point to the same causal property.
- Allan Gibbard (norm-expressivism — E3): A causal process operates in the world to produce our affective response mechanisms, and this process results in our good.

both sides.[1] My strategy in defending prescriptive realism will be to start with a brief description of what I see as the least concessive positions, namely the platonist and the emotivist positions, and then to work inwards, so to speak, by describing the successive concessions that have been made from each side. Once all these concessions have been made, we will have a position that can be called either expressivist or realist or a hybrid of the two. I am going to claim that we will have preserved the truths seen on both sides. We will also have a position that will help us understand God's role in human morality.

1. Platonism: G. E. Moore

G. E. Moore's *Principia Ethica*, first published in 1903, is an obvious place to begin a consideration of moral realism in twentieth-century

---

1. My position is "quietist," to use a term from Simon Blackburn, who talks of the "quietist" view urged by R. M. Hare "that no real issue can be built around the objectivity or otherwise of moral values." See "Errors and the Phenomenology of Value," in *Essays in Quasi-Realism* (Oxford: Oxford University Press, 1993), p. 153. But R. M. Hare has not made all the necessary concessions, in my view, to remove issues of substance between the parties. Thus he says, "Think of one world into whose fabric values are objectively built; and think of another in which those values have been annihilated. And remember that in both worlds the people in them go on being concerned about the same things — there is no difference in the 'subjective' concern which people have for things, only in their 'objective' value. Now I ask, 'What is the difference between the states of affairs in these two worlds?' Can any answer be given except 'None whatever'?" (Quoted in J. L. Mackie, *Ethics: Inventing Right and Wrong* [Harmondsworth: Penguin, 1977], p. 21.) But from the realist perspective this is like saying that there is no difference between two worlds in which people have the same beliefs, but in one world the things that correspond to those beliefs have been annihilated. In other words, only a person who already accepts that it does not make sense to talk of the existence of values in the things outside us *rather than* in our evaluation of them will accept the claim that there is no difference between the two worlds in question.

analytic ethics, since he set the terms for much of the subsequent discussion. Intrinsic goodness is, Moore thinks, a real property of things, even though it does not exist in time and is not the object of sense perception. It is in both of these ways like the number two. Moore explicitly aligns himself here with Plato and against the class of empiricist philosophers, "to which," he says, "most Englishmen have belonged."[2] Goodness is objective, in the sense that it is there independently of us (though not in space and time). To call something good is to evaluate, and to point to a value property — the goodness which the thing has. His predecessors, Moore thinks, have almost all committed the error, which he calls "the naturalistic fallacy," of trying to define this value property by identifying it with a non-evaluative property. For example, they have proposed that goodness is pleasure, or what produces pleasure. But whatever non-evaluative property we try to say goodness is identical to, we will find that it remains an open question whether that property is in fact good.[3] For example, if we say that goodness is identical with pleasure, we will find that it still makes sense to ask whether pleasure is good. This is true also if we propose a supernatural property for the identity with goodness, for example the property of being commanded by God. It still makes sense to ask whether what God commands is good. This question cannot be the same as the question "Is

2. G. E. Moore, *Principia Ethica* (1903; Cambridge: Cambridge University Press, 1993), p. 162.

3. There are different versions of the fallacy in *Principia Ethica,* and the thesis can also easily be trivialized. Moore quotes Butler, "Everything is what it is, and not another thing," as a way to sum up what is wrong with the naturalistic fallacy. But the naturalists are not claiming that the defining natural characteristics they propose are "another thing." The general problem here is to understand what is supposed to happen in a philosophical analysis, as Plato saw at *Meno* 80d. Moore's point can be confined more narrowly to the claim that goodness cannot be identified with any of the natural or metaphysical properties with which it has been identified in the tradition of ethical theory within which Moore is working. See R. M. Hare, *The Language of Morals* (Oxford: Oxford University Press, 1961), pp. 86-93.

what God commands what God commands?" which is not still an open question. But if these questions are different, then the two properties, goodness and being commanded by God, cannot be the same, and to say (by way of a definition) that they are the same is to commit the fallacy. Intrinsic goodness, Moore says, is a simple non-natural property and indefinable. To say that it is non-natural is to distinguish it both from natural properties (like producing pleasure) and supernatural ones (like being commanded by God).

It may seem mysterious how humans can have access to non-natural properties. How does Moore think that we know what is good? The answer is that we know it by a special form of cognition, which he calls "intuition." By this he means that the access is not based on an inference or argument, but is self-evident (though we can still get it wrong, just as we can with sense perception).[4] Moore thinks the way to determine what things have positive value intrinsically is to consider what things are such that, if they existed *by themselves,* in absolute isolation, we should yet judge their existence to be good.[5] By reflecting on this question, together with a group of like-minded souls, he reached the conclusion that "by far the most valuable things, which we know or can imagine, are certain states of consciousness, which may be roughly described as the pleasures of human intercourse and the enjoyment of beautiful objects."

Standardly, Moore thinks, our wills join together organically the cognition or intuition of goodness and something non-cognitive like a desire.[6] I say "standardly" because Moore thinks it is possible to have the cognition without the non-cognitive element. This may be clearer in a more limited example, the beautiful. One of my col-

---

4. The intuition is not the same as the person's report that she has the intuition, and to identify the two is an example of the naturalistic fallacy. See also Henry Sidgwick, *The Methods of Ethics* (London: Macmillan, 1874), p. 211. Sidgwick also denies that what he calls "intuitions" are infallible.

5. Moore, *Principia Ethica*, p. 234.

6. "Something else beside the thinking a thing good" (Moore, *Principia Ethica*, p. 186).

leagues suggested the example of a velvet painting of Elvis. I can distinguish the cognition of the beautiful qualities of the thing (say, its raw animal power) and the emotions caused in me by this cognition (say, my swoon). The cognition of these objects has little value, Moore says, apart from the appropriate emotions, and the emotions have little value apart from the cognition of the appropriate objects; but it *is* nonetheless possible to have the cognition without the emotion. Separate from both of these is the judgment that the painting deserves to cause the emotion, which Moore calls, following Kant, the judgment of taste.[7] So we have three elements here; the cognition, the emotion, and the judgment. These same distinctions can be made about the good more broadly, and I will return to them.

2. Emotivism: A. J. Ayer

A. J. Ayer starts from a logical positivist criterion for meaningful statements, which has the effect that ethical statements are *not* meaningful.[8] Since I don't think logical positivism is defensible, I will not go into this further. But in order to say what we *are* doing in making ethical judgments, Ayer is led to emphasize and analyze further the non-cognitive ingredient in evaluation which Moore identified. And here he makes a characteristic expressivist move. Suppose I say to a cannibal, "You acted wrongly in eating your prisoner." Ayer thinks I am not *stating* anything more than if I had simply said, "You ate your prisoner." I am, rather, evincing my moral disapproval of it. It is as if I had said, "You ate your prisoner" in a peculiar tone of horror, or written it with the addition of some special exclamation marks. These do not add anything to the literal meaning of the sentence, he thinks. They merely serve to show that the expression of it

---

7. Moore, *Principia Ethica,* pp. 238, 247-48, 259.

8. A. J. Ayer, *Language, Truth and Logic* (London: Gollancz, 1936), pp. 107-8. I could also have used here Charles Stevenson's *Ethics and Language* (New Haven: Yale University Press, 1944).

is attended by certain feelings in the speaker. Ayer claims that the function of the ethical words is purely "emotive," meaning that they are used to express feeling about certain objects, but not to make any assertion about them. Sometimes this is caricatured as "the yah/ boo" theory of evaluation; as though we could say what we mean by "You acted wrongly in eating your prisoner" by saying "You ate your prisoner. Boo!"

This account is, Ayer says, a kind of subjectivism. It is not the kind of subjectivist view that sees moral judgments as *reports* of our feelings, but as *expressions* of our feelings. Moore pointed out, quite correctly in Ayer's view, that if ethical statements *were* simply statements about the speaker's feelings, it would be impossible to disagree about questions of value. There is no dispute between person A's report that he (that is, person A) approves of eating prisoners and person B's report that she (that is, person B) does not. Since Moore held it to be obvious that we do disagree about such questions, he concluded that this kind of subjectivism is false. Unfortunately for Ayer, he has to concede that his own kind of subjectivism leads to the same result, that it is impossible to disagree about questions of value. On Ayer's view of moral judgment, "Eating people is bad" and "Eating people is good" do not express propositions at all, and therefore cannot express inconsistent propositions. This is an embarrassment to Ayer, and he has to say that when we think we are disputing about questions of value, we are actually disputing about the non-evaluative facts of the case which lie behind our attitudes (for example, facts about the likely consequences of cannibalism).

3. Prescriptivism: R. M. Hare

R. M. Hare's prescriptivism preserves the emotivist distinction between moral judgment and statement or assertion, but he insists that this distinction is consistent with the objectivity of moral judgment. He was a prisoner of war of the Japanese in World War II, and it was important to him to find a way of talking about morality that did allow both disputes about questions of moral value and then rational agreement about them. He thought that the world would be a better place if this structure could be laid out and used as the basis for moral education and the settling of moral disagreements. His idea was to hang on to the kind of objectivity that Immanuel Kant described. I will be returning to Kant in the third chapter. The idea is that the person making the moral judgment can abstract from any partiality towards herself, by eliminating all reference to individuals, including herself, from the judgment. If moral judgments, like scientific laws, are always about a *type* of situation, then she is not allowed in making such a judgment to make essential reference to herself. If it is right for her to eat her prisoner, then it is right for anyone in her type of situation; and this includes the hypothetical situation in which she happens to be the missionary and her present prisoner happens to be the cannibal. This is what I will call "the first expressivist concession" (E1), that morality is objective in this Kantian way.[9] Hare also emphasizes that moral judgment is prescriptive, expressing the will. He observes that not all utterances which have the surface grammar of assertions are in fact to be analyzed as such. He calls "descriptivism" the mistake of being misled by the surface grammar into thinking of evaluative judgment as a species of assertion.[10] Suppose I judge sincerely that I ought to do ac-

9. See R. M. Hare, *The Language of Morals,* pp. 16 and 70. See also "Could Kant Have Been a Utilitarian?" *Utilitas* 5, no. 1 (1993): 1-16.

10. The mistake derives from what John Austin called "the descriptive fallacy," appealing in turn to Kant. "It has come to be commonly held that many utterances which look like statements are either not intended at all, or only intended in part, to record or impart straightforward information about the facts: for example, 'ethical propositions' are perhaps intended, solely or partly, to evince emotion or to prescribe conduct or to influence it in special ways. Here too KANT was among the pioneers" (Austin, *How to Do Things with Words* [Oxford: Oxford University Press, 1965], p. 3). Charles Stevenson was already moving in the prescriptivist direction, adding to the view that evaluative judgment expresses emotion the claim that it includes a prescription to others to

tion A in circumstances C. Prescriptivism analyzes my judgment in terms of a universal prescription that I am committed to, of the form "Let anyone like me in the relevant respects do an action like A in the relevant respects in circumstances like C in the relevant respects." In Kant's terms this is to will the maxim of my action as a universal law.

Prescriptivism is helpfully seen as a response to Moore's claim that goodness is indefinable. Hare agrees that there is indeed something about the way we use the word "good" which makes it impossible to hold the sort of position Moore was attacking. But he thinks Moore did not see clearly what this something was; we use the word "good" to commend.[11] To commend something is always to commend it *for* having certain characteristics, which give us what Hare calls the "criteria" of the judgment. The strawberry is good because it meets the criterion of sweetness. Hare introduced into twentieth-century discussion the term "supervenience" to describe the relation between commending something and the facts on which the commending relies. The term is actually far older, and I will be focusing in the second chapter on its use in a similar context by John Duns Scotus.[12] Hare explains the relation (for value judgments) like this. Value properties supervene on non-value properties, and that means that things have the value properties because they have the non-value properties. For example, a strawberry is good because it is sweet. But the value property is not the same as the non-value property, and ascribing the second does not entail ascribing the first.[13] *If*

---

feel similarly. Before his death, he told R. M. Hare that if he were starting again, he would do the analysis of moral judgment in terms of universal prescriptions.

11. R. M. Hare, *The Language of Morals,* pp. 83-84.

12. See Scotus, *Quodlibet* q.18, in Allan B. Wolter, trans., *Duns Scotus on the Will and Morality* (Washington: Catholic University of America Press, 1986), p. 169.

13. R. M. Hare, *Sorting Out Ethics* (Oxford: Clarendon Press, 1997), p. 21. It is this supervenience relation that explains what Moore was after in insisting

I judge, however, that a strawberry is good because it is sweet and firm and juicy, I am committed to the same evaluation of any other strawberry with just those non-evaluative properties.[14] Let us call the non-evaluative property here "the subvening base." We can now show that dispute is possible about value questions, a possibility which A. J. Ayer felt he strictly had to deny. For prescriptions can conflict. "Shut the door" and "Do not shut the door" are opposed in very much the same way as "The door is shut" and "The door is not shut." Indeed it is the same state of affairs, the door's being shut, that both satisfies the first of the two commands and makes true the first of the two statements. If two people disagree about the criteria for goodness in strawberries, they can agree that a strawberry is sweet and disagree about whether it is good. Two people can make opposite prescriptions about the same subvening base.

Moreover, prescriptivism allows for the disputes to be *rational*. The prescriptivist account of moral judgment requires a kind of rational screening of what we are thinking of doing. This screening is much like Kant's procedure with the Categorical Imperative to screen maxims for action.[15] We can think of this screening as required for endorsement from a particular vantage point, what Hare

on a necessary connection between the intrinsic goodness of a thing and the thing itself, even though the intrinsic goodness is not a *part* of the thing.

14. It is this conditionality that lies behind the claim Simon Blackburn makes that the supervenience relation including lack of entailment from the subvening base requires expressivism for its intelligibility. See "Moral Realism," in *Morality and Moral Reasoning*, ed. John Casey (London: Methuen, 1973).

15. I am not going to discuss here two questions about prescriptivism which a fuller treatment would cover. The first is whether the universalization procedure illegitimately blocks some of our concerns which are basic to human life. See Bernard Williams, *Ethics and the Limits of Philosophy* (Cambridge, Mass.: Harvard University Press, 1985), pp. 89-92, and John E. Hare, *The Moral Gap* (Oxford: Clarendon Press, 1996), pp. 150-59. The second is whether it admits personal ideals that morality should exclude (for instance, the Nazi's ideal of racial purity). See Allan Gibbard, "Hare's Analysis of 'Ought' and Its Implications," in *Hare and Critics,* ed. Douglas Seanor and N. Fotion (Oxford: Clarendon Press, 1988), pp. 57-72.

calls the position of the archangel, who has complete information and complete impartiality. The question we need to ask is: Would the archangel endorse this action? The archangel knows the preferences of all the affected parties. He knows how much the cannibal wants to eat and how much the missionary wants not to be eaten. And the archangel is completely impartial between these two parties. It is not that we in fact occupy this position, but that this is the vantage point we are trying to approximate in making moral judgments. This is how we can be rational in our moral decisions. The archangel is a model of objectivity in the sense that the prescriptivist wants to preserve it.

4. Humble Platonism: Iris Murdoch

Iris Murdoch is a platonist about ethics who takes R. M. Hare as one of her prime initial opponents.[16] I want to isolate one concession she makes, which takes her some distance from the position of G. E. Moore. The concession is that human beings are by nature selfish. I will call this "the first realist concession" (R1). It is a concession to subjectivity in that she recognizes and indeed stresses that accurate moral perception needs obedience, a selfless attention, a pure heart; but our moral thinking is in fact usually characterized by the opposite of these — by the root inclination to favor ourselves unjustly. She is a platonist about value, but with an Augustinian rather than a platonist view of the heart. Moore agrees that humans are capable of great evil. But he has no equivalent to what Murdoch calls "the fat

16. I could have chosen Philippa Foot in this section, perhaps under the label "descriptivist," as someone on the realist side of the dispute who takes R. M. Hare as her prime initial target. Murdoch has the advantage, for my purposes, of being closer to Moore both in her platonism and in the centrality she gives to aesthetic beauty. Her writing is also inspiring, in a way that the moral philosophy of the twentieth century is often not. Unfortunately I will not be able to give much of a flavor of this in what follows.

relentless ego," which corrupts our nature at its root. This concession has far-reaching consequences for Murdoch's views. It means that our access to the good is always precarious and incomplete, and we are always fatally prone to self-deception. It also motivates her central objection to prescriptivism, which is that if the will is corrupt in this way, then it cannot be the creative source of good. To make sense of this objection, I need to explain how she sees the history here, though I think she is wrong in her account both of Kant and of R. M. Hare. Kant, she says, abolished God and made man God in His stead. In fact, she thinks Kant's man had received a glorious incarnation almost a century before Kant in the work of Milton: "His proper name," she says, "is Lucifer."[17] Murdoch sets up a contrast here between pride and humility. The existentialist and Anglo-Saxon heirs of Kant (such as Sartre in France and R. M. Hare in England) make the human will the creator of value, which was previously seen as inscribed in the heavens. Murdoch thinks this is merely a surrender to self-importance. What we need to recover, she says, is the sense of value as a magnetic source outside our wills, to which our wills respond if we are disciplined in virtue and especially in the virtue of humility. She distinguishes two kinds of freedom. There is the fictitious kind of freedom that existentialists and, so she says, prescriptivists extol, the imposition of value onto a value-free world.

17. Iris Murdoch, *The Sovereignty of Good over Other Concepts* (Cambridge: Cambridge University Press, 1967), p. 4. This view of Kant is highly questionable. See John E. Hare, *The Moral Gap,* chapters two and three. Her view of R. M. Hare is also wrong. In talking of "decisions of principle" (in *The Language of Morals,* pp. 56f.) he did not mean that humans are creators of value. His point was that in cases like Sartre's famous example of the young Frenchman who has to decide whether to look after his aged mother or go off to fight in the resistance, an agent may have reached an end of looking at reasons for and against and still have no verdict. Then he simply has to decide. There will be reasons from inside a way of life, which can then guide him. But there may not be answers to his initial agonizing question, "Why should I choose this way of life?" See also Peter Byrne, *The Moral Interpretation of Religion* (Edinburgh: Edinburgh University Press, 1998), p. 100.

And then there is the freedom that comes from humility. Freedom of this second kind is not just chucking one's weight about; it is the disciplined overcoming of self. Humility is not just self-effacement, rather like having an inaudible voice; it is selfless respect for reality.[18] One primary example for Murdoch, as for Moore, is the contemplation of something beautiful, which can have the effect of "unselfing" the contemplator, so that she attends entirely to the object. The same kind of thing can happen with intellectual disciplines, like learning a foreign language, which can take me (if I love it) towards something which is alien to me, which I cannot take over or control. This is, finally, what can happen when I love another person, with this sustained kind of attention. The Good, Murdoch says, unifies all these fragmentary experiences of value into a whole that transcends us. It is a "magnetic center," to which we feel the attraction but which we never reach.

There is an aspect of Murdoch's thought which is hard to fit with her talk of a "magnetic center." She holds that human life has no external point or *telos*. She thinks Christianity panders to us by claiming to give us a guarantee that the good will in the end prevail. But the effect of her denial is to make the Good completely inert, contrary to Plato, for whom the human world is neither aimless nor self-contained. The Forms for him, and especially the Form of the Good, have a causal role as well as an epistemological one. I do not myself see how to reconcile Murdoch's talk about aimlessness with the talk about a magnetic center. The former claim can be muted by supposing that she means merely to deny an external *mind* controlling the universe, or the latter claim can be muted by attributing to her the view that we should live *as if* there were a magnetic center, even though there is no such thing. But neither of these interpretations fits at all well what she actually says.[19]

18. Murdoch, *The Sovereignty of Good,* p. 26.
19. See *The Fire and the Sun* (Oxford: Oxford University Press, 1977), p. 65, and *Metaphysics as a Guide to Morals* (Harmondsworth: Penguin, 1993), p. 464. See

Murdoch connects the idea of a magnetic center with Plato's allegory of the cave, from which we emerge to look up at the sun. "It is *difficult* to look at the sun: it is not like looking at other things. We somehow retain the idea, and art both expresses and symbolizes it, that the lines really do converge. There is a magnetic center. But it is easier to look at the converging edges than to look at the center itself. We do not and probably cannot know, conceptualize, what it is like in the center."[20] She goes on to warn that it is fatally easy to confuse the sun with the fire inside the cave, which represents (she says) "the self, the old unregenerate psyche, that great source of energy and warmth." Here we are back to the fat relentless ego. "The fire may be mistaken for the sun, and self-scrutiny taken for goodness." I think she is right (though the interpretation of Plato is probably wrong). As soon as we try to say what it is like in the center, we fall prey to self-aggrandizement. Given that our nature is selfish, it may be that certain things attract us (for example, power and prestige) in a way that is not in fact good. I will suggest later that Aristotle's theory is a good test case. Power and prestige are, in his system, essential parts of the chief good for human beings. Aristotle is not wrong to say that we do naturally pursue these things, but he is wrong to argue that because we naturally pursue them they are good. If we try to argue to the character of the good from the character of our emotions and desires, we are likely to fall into this danger that Murdoch identifies as mistaking the fire for the sun, or mistaking self-scrutiny for the discovery of goodness.

Murdoch says that humans are by nature selfish, and she therefore holds that our evaluative knowledge is precarious and incomplete. It is precarious because we are always fatally liable to

---

also Byrne, *The Moral Interpretation of Religion,* pp. 112f. The question of how to understand Murdoch here is at issue between Scott Dunbar, "On Art, Morals and Religion: Some Reflections on the Work of Iris Murdoch," *Religious Studies* 14 (1978): 515-24; Basil Mitchell, *Morality: Religious and Secular* (Oxford: Clarendon Press, 1980), pp. 64-72; and G. Graham, "Spiritualised Morality and Traditional Religion," *Ratio* 9 NS (1996): 78-84.

20. Murdoch, *The Sovereignty of Good,* pp. 32-33.

self-deception and false comfort. It is incomplete because, as she holds, the good is a unity or magnetic center, and we are always fragmented to various degrees. She thinks very differently from G. E. Moore about how the good is to be apprehended. We can imagine Moore's group seated together with furrowed brows, concentrating on the required thought experiments about what things would still be good in absolute isolation. For Murdoch, in contrast, the process of apprehension is one of lifelong obedience, mortification, and self-discipline. The reason this is needed is our tendency to self-indulgence, and the attendant corruption of even our reflective processes by self-gratifying fantasies.[21]

But neither Kant nor the prescriptivists are creative anti-realists in the way Murdoch proposes. I will make this point about Kant in the third chapter. Prescriptivism is more correctly seen as an additional reason for the humility Murdoch extols. To see this, we should first separate two different things that occur in our evaluations. There is first the experience of the magnetic force that Murdoch describes. But secondly, this response is endorsed in an evaluative judgment. To see the genealogy of this distinction, it is helpful to go back again to Moore. Moore distinguished within an evaluation between something cognitive, which is *thinking* something good, something *non-cognitive* like an emotion, and separately from both of these the *judging* that a thing is good. In the case of seeing something beautiful, this is the distinction between recognizing the raw animal power of the image of Elvis, the swoon, and finally the judgment of taste. I think this account is basically right, but can be improved by supplementing it with Robert Roberts's account of emotion.[22] Not all value judgments are based on emotions, but emotions provide one central case. Roberts understands the emotions as

21. Murdoch, *Metaphysics as a Guide to Morals,* pp. 501-3: "The inhibition of unworthy fantasies is perhaps the most accessible discipline."

22. Robert C. Roberts, "What an Emotion Is: A Sketch," *Philosophical Review* 97 (1988): 183-209. The view is developed in the second chapter of *The Schooled Heart: An Essay in Moral Psychology,* forthcoming.

concern-based construals. A construal is a "seeing-as." Roberts gives the analogy of looking at an ambiguous figure that can be seen as an old woman looking forward or as a young woman looking backward (see above). The two organizations of the lines in the figure are imposed by the viewing subject; but they are not *sheer* subjectivity. The subject discovers something that is already there in the drawing. To fear something is to construe it ("see" it) as a danger or other bad possibility. Consider the following example, which Roberts has given me. A mother fears that her son may start sleeping with his girlfriend. Her fear consists, according to Roberts, in her construal of the situation as containing this bad possibility. But to construe the possibility as *bad* (that is, to feel the emotion of fear) requires that she care about what this possibility involves or impinges on — in this case, the sexual purity of her son. Many mothers see the possibility of their sons' sleeping with their girlfriends but without fearing it/ seeing it as bad, because they don't care about sexual behavior in this

16

traditional way. So we see something corresponding to the first two elements in Moore's analysis of an evaluation: the seeing-as (the "thought") and the caring (the "non-cognitive element"). But the example also illustrates the necessity of the third element. We can imagine a mother who is jittery about her son's chastity, but who has come to believe that there is really nothing wrong with extra-marital sexual activity. She considers her emotion an irrational hangover from her upbringing. By contrast, the mother in our example endorses her emotion; she regards it as appropriate and fitting to the situation. Without this endorsement, her emotion is not what I will call a full-blooded value judgment.

Now we can return to Murdoch's humility. If we separate these three elements, the construal and the desire and the endorsement, we can see how expressivism can give us an additional reason for humility. Because of our selfishness, the construals and desires present in emotion are biased towards the self. But value judgment according to the expressivist also requires endorsement, and our selfishness will also incline us to endorse what is not impartially good. Where our treasure is, there shall our *heart* be also. Murdoch mistakenly condemns the prescriptivist for false pride, for putting the moral agent in the god-displacing role of creating value by her own will. But this is not the prescriptivist's intention. Indeed, for the prescriptivist this is just another form of descriptivism, his opponent's invariable mistake. The realist thinks of values as existing things in the world, like armadillos, and condemns the prescriptivist for thinking of them as existing things in the world put there by us, like armchairs. The central expressivist point is, rather, that to make a value judgment is not *merely* to respond to something out there in the world, but to endorse or deliberately to withhold endorsement from such a response. What we are inclined to endorse will depend on our fundamental reflective loyalties. If it is the case that we are born, as Kant thought, with an innate tendency to prefer our own happiness to our duty, then this hierarchy will be reflected in the endorsements we naturally make. Murdoch talks about "the fat relentless ego," and Kant about "the dear self." But the essential point is the same.

5. Error Theory: J. L. Mackie

The second expressivist concession (E2) is made by the error theory of J. L. Mackie, and it is a concession about the meaning of value language.[23] Mackie says that although the prescriptivist is right to

23. I could also have used here the "quasi-realism" of Simon Blackburn. Both Blackburn and Mackie are "projectivists" about value. The difference is that Blackburn wants to emphasize the sense in which value judgments are nonetheless "true," and we can have knowledge of value. He explains the point of quasi-realism by using P. F. Strawson's distinction between a "genetic-psychological" theory, which gives an account of the development of a concept through social history or individual growth, and an "analytic-philosophical" theory, which is concerned to capture the structure of the mature, adult experience. So there may be a genetic account of our creation or projection of value into the world as a result of social or psychological pressures of various kinds. But the analytic account must "leave everything as it is." Blackburn says, "To put it bluntly, we have created something that involves us essentially in the cognitive: in judgement, reason, truth, fact. . . . The projectivist is, or should be, perfectly happy with what I call 'the propositional surface' of ethics; he does not suppose that in ordinary thought there is a constant theoretical commentary busy explaining and justifying the use of propositional forms." See "The Flight to Reality," in *Virtues and Reasons,* ed. Rosalind Hurst-house et al. (Oxford: Clarendon Press, 1995), pp. 53-54. The claim that expressivists can hold on to the *truth* of evaluative judgment is also in prescriptivism. See R. M. Hare, *Sorting Out Ethics,* p. 56: "I hope [I have] shown how little grasp of these issues those people have who think (as many beginner students are taught to think) that it is sufficient to distinguish between what they call cognitivist and non-cognitivist theories by saying that they give opposing answers to the question 'Can moral statements be true or false?' The answer to this question is that they can, but that the important issue between descriptivists and non-descriptivists is not settled thereby." Both Blackburn and Hare are therefore cognitivists in the sense that they believe in the possible truth of moral judgments. Hare does not however suppose, like both Mackie and Blackburn, that our moral judgment is *creative* of moral value.

stress the prescriptivity of value language, he is wrong about what ordinary people mean when they use the value terms. Mackie's view is that ordinary value judgment does not merely claim to be "objective" in a Kantian sense; it also claims to pick out features that are parts of the fabric of the world, and are there independently of us. This is the second concession. Mackie is conceding this point about meaning to the platonist. But he goes on to argue that nothing *can* be both prescriptive and objective in this sense at the same time. This is why his theory is an error theory. He thinks that ordinary moral judgment, like ordinary sensory judgment, is making claims that are false. Mackie thinks that when we ordinarily judge that something is red, we are making a claim that the color as we see it literally belongs to the surface of the colored object. But this claim, says Mackie, is false.[24] The reason we fall into this error, both with colors and values, is that we project or objectify. As Hume says, the mind spreads itself on external objects. Mackie says that we have the experience of desiring things, and calling "good" what satisfies the desires. But we reach the notion of something's being *objectively* good, or having intrinsic value, by reversing the direction of dependence here, by making the desire depend upon the goodness, instead of the goodness on the desire. We have the perfectly respectable idea of the objective features of a thing that make it desirable (the sweetness of the strawberry, for example), and then we confuse this with the idea that the desirability is itself an objective feature in the same sense. Mackie thinks the idea of objective prescriptivity did make sense when people believed in a divine lawgiver, who both existed independently of us and gave us authoritative commands. But, Mackie thinks, this belief has now faded out, and the idea of objective prescriptivity de-

---

24. "Naive realism about colours might be a correct analysis not only of our pre-scientific colour concepts but also of the conventional meanings of colour words, and even of the meanings with which scientifically sophisticated people use them when they are off their guard, and yet it might not be a correct account of the status of the colours." J. L. Mackie, *Ethics: Inventing Right and Wrong,* p. 20.

serves to fade out with it. This idea of objective prescriptivity is the center of my own view, what I call prescriptive realism. The difference between Mackie and me is that he thinks this is an error and I think it is the truth.

He gives two main arguments why nothing can be both prescriptive and objective in his sense at the same time. The first is the argument from relativity, that people's moral beliefs are just too different from each other for us to think they have a single source in some objective good. This is an important argument, and I will come back to it in the next section. The second argument is that objective prescriptivity makes values into a very odd kind of entity. This argument is a response to the platonist position, and indeed Mackie puts forward Plato's Ideas or Forms as his prime candidates for what objective values would have to be like if there were any. Mackie finds such things metaphysically peculiar. Plato's Form of the Good both tells the person who knows it what to do and makes him do it.[25] Mackie finds strange here a certain conjunction. What is mysterious is not so much that the good authoritatively tells a person what to do, or that it causally makes a person do something; but it is the conjunction of these two powers in a single item that mystifies him.[26] How *can* the telling and the making go together in this way?

I want to propose that we lose the sense of strangeness Mackie felt

25. "The Form of the Good is such that knowledge of it provides the knower with both a direction and an overriding motive; something's being good both tells the person who knows this to pursue it and makes him pursue it. An objective good would be sought by anyone who was acquainted with it, not because of any contingent fact that this person, or every person, is so constituted that he desires this end, but just because the end has to-be-pursuedness somehow built into it." J. L. Mackie, *Ethics: Inventing Right and Wrong*, p. 40.

26. This is one reason why the lucky few, in Plato's allegory of the cave, who have come out of the cave and finally looked up at the sun can be relied upon to go back into the cave (even though they would love to stay contemplating) in order to help bring others out. They have been caused to go back by seeing the Form.

if we separate the two features of "objective prescriptivity" he combined together. I think we can see how these two features, the telling and the making, are both operating in a value judgment, but operating at different moments in it. And we can go on to mark out a middle ground between expressivism and realism, a ground that I announced as "prescriptive realism" at the beginning of the chapter. On this middle ground we can say, first, that there is a "magnetic" or "repulsive force" attaching to things that is itself part of the fabric of the world (this is Mackie's *making*). "Magnetic force" is a perfectly natural way to describe a causal power, though Mackie has a restrictive notion of causation which makes this kind of cause hard to accept. We are given motivation by certain features of what we experience. For example, food attracts us when we are hungry. I mean the term "motivation" to cover desire and concern and emotional attraction and repulsion in general.[27] I do not think we need to suppose (like Moore) that this magnetic (or repulsive) force is a *simple* property, the same in all things we experience as good (or bad). The property in the thing and its effect on us may both be extremely complex, and there may be many different varieties. We find the storm terrifying, the cruelty disgusting, the portrait intriguing. The search for a single simple property here to explain all such experience is probably a mistake, and has led to a bogus sense of mystery about what this property could possibly be. Consider, for example, the sense of vertigo when on the edge of a cliff, and the strange mixture of dread of the abyss and a pull towards it. Why should this kind of mixture be present anywhere else? My point at the moment is just that there may be many qualitatively different complexes of "magnetic" or "repulsive" properties in the thing and different qualities of response in us.

Value judgment expresses, however, not only an affective response, on my view, but separately the element that I have called endorsement (this is Mackie's *telling*). To judge that a thing is good is

---

27. English is lacking the generic term *orexis* which Greek possesses, and which I appealed to in the introduction.

not merely to report the magnetic force, but to judge that the thing *deserves* to have that effect on us.[28] We are deliberately submitting to what we are claiming as authoritative. Endorsement is an autonomous submission. A good analogy here is Kant's remark that we should recognize our duties as God's commands.[29] I will return to this in chapter three. Kant is also committed to the autonomy of moral judgment, and it might seem that his remark is inconsistent with this commitment. But it is not. Consider the case of submission to *political* authority. This can be autonomous, for Kant, if the political authority makes possible a political realm in which external freedom is respected, for the moral agent values this freedom as the outward expression of an internal freedom that she values as constitutive of the moral law itself. In the same way, submission to God's commands can be autonomous if God's authority is seen to make possible a kingdom of ends in which all members are respected as ends in themselves. The moral agent's attachment to the kingdom of ends is constitutive of her moral character, and there is nothing heteronomous about such an attachment. So there can be an autonomous acknowledgment of the force of some value recognized as external to the agent. We can acknowledge autonomously the force of some value recognized as external to us.

Murdoch's postulation of a magnetic *center* is germane here. To endorse a response to some felt attraction is to acknowledge a con-

---

28. McDowell puts this point in terms of a disanalogy between value and color. "The disanalogy is that a virtue (say) is conceived to be not merely such as to elicit the appropriate 'attitude' (as a colour is merely such as to cause the appropriate experiences), but rather such as to *merit* it." See "Values as Secondary Qualities," *Morality and Objectivity,* ed. Ted Honderich (London: Routledge & Kegan Paul, 1985), p. 175. See also Charles Taylor, *Sources of the Self* (Cambridge, Mass.: Harvard University Press, 1989), p. 6. Taylor points to the difference between feeling nauseated and the respect for persons; the persons *merit* and are perceived as meriting the respect, whereas the feeling of nausea is merely causal.

29. For example, *KpV* V, 130 (but there are similar remarks throughout the corpus).

sistency between this magnetic force and the force of the Good as a whole. Consider the case of the Milgram experiments on obedience, in which roughly two thirds of the subjects ended up doing all they were ordered to do (believing they were administering electric shocks of increasing severity, that might eventually even be lethal, to another subject).[30] We need to distinguish accepting a norm from being in the grip of a norm, in the way these subjects were in the grip of the norm that prescribed following directions. What is the difference? Accepting a norm is a result of the workings of the demand for consistency in one's life as a whole and in the positions one adopts. The subjects in Milgram's experiments did not in this sense accept the norms they were following, and one sign of this was their remorse and subsequent anger.[31] But there are different levels and stages of endorsement, and I have discussed them elsewhere. Endorsement is expressed most clearly in the judgment that the emotion or desire fits the situation that occasioned it. But an agent can endorse or withhold endorsement at different stages of reflective distance from her initial affective response. First, take the case of forgiveness. The victim may endorse the anger she feels at the offender in the sense that she judges that the anger is appropriate to the offense. But she may decide, nonetheless, that she wants not to feel that anger any longer, and she wants reconciliation. This is different from the case where she decides that her anger was disproportionate to the offense. When she decides to forgive, she is deciding not to endorse the anger, and not to endorse that part of her character which is disposed to hold on to the anger. Another similar case is the person who is constantly in situations calling for intense emotion. A surgeon has to get used to the fact that life is at stake in her smallest

30. I take the case and the analysis from Gibbard, *Wise Choices, Apt Feelings* (Cambridge, Mass.: Harvard University Press, 1990), p. 58.
31. Endorsing a desire needs to be distinguished from acknowledging it and identifying with it. See John E. Hare, *The Moral Gap*, pp. 118-28. Endorsement can be either occurrent or dispositional, where it will often operate in default mode.

actions. The anxiety this naturally arouses is perfectly fitting, but she has to refuse endorsement of it, and be grateful for the gradual numbing that often accompanies professional practice. Quite generally, an emotion or desire may be held to fit a situation but may be overridden in an evaluative judgment.[32] If I am sending my aged mother to a nursing home, a feeling of guilt (with its attendant concern and construal) may be perfectly fitting. She nurtured me in my state of dependency, and now I am refusing to do the same for her. But I may decide that the situation as a whole (including the needs of the rest of my family) requires me morally to override this feeling. I need a normative theory to tell me when this is. I may even endorse being the sort of person who feels guilt in such a situation, but I do not finally endorse action in accordance with this feeling. The agent who endorses or withholds endorsement in an evaluative judgment is not stepping outside her character when she passes judgment. But she is trying to hold herself open (to attend, as Murdoch puts it) to all the relevant facts and to the other people involved, so that her character can be corrected of any unhelpful biases.

Prescriptive realism is like the other forms of expressivism in that it insists on the prescriptive character of moral judgment. Standardly I am, in making such a judgment about an action, telling myself to do something, and expressing my will. But the view is also realist, in that it holds there is a pull coming from outside me which I acknowledge in such a judgment. Most of the realists I am referring to in this paper deny themselves this middle ground. They treat moral judgments as being pure members of the cognitive category of mental states (such as beliefs); and they say it is expressivists who include essential reference to the agent's non-cognitive mental states (such as desires or will). Thus Mark Platts quotes G. E. M. Anscombe's distinction between two different directions of fit between mental states and the world: "Beliefs aim at the true, and their being

32. R. M. Hare distinguishes here between intuitive and critical levels of thinking; see *Moral Thinking* (Oxford: Clarendon Press, 1981), pp. 44-64.

true is their fitting the world; falsity is a decisive failing in a belief, and false beliefs should be discarded; beliefs should be changed to fit the world, not *vice versa*. Desires aim at realization, and their realization is the world fitting with them; the fact that the indicative content of a desire is not realised in the world is not yet a failing *in the desire,* and not yet any reason to discard the desire; the world, crudely, should be changed to fit with our desires, not *vice versa*." Platts then says, "The point is that the realist treats moral judgements as being PURE members of the first cognitive category of mental states [i.e., beliefs] and that the anti-realist claims that any full specification of a reason for action must make reference to the (potential) agent's mental states of the second category" [i.e., desires].[33] As far as I can see, this allocation is arbitrary.

6. Disposition Theory: John McDowell

John McDowell accepts from Mackie the analogy between values and colors, but disagrees with him about the proper account of both of them.[34] He makes what I am going to call the "second realist concession" (R2), that values do not have to be seen as real independently of general human dispositions to respond to them in a certain way in appropriate circumstances.[35] McDowell's view of color is that an

33. Mark Platts, *Ways of Meaning* (London: Routledge & Kegan Paul, 1979), p. 257; see also chapters 10, 13. See also Richard Boyd, "How to Be a Moral Realist," in *Essays on Moral Realism,* ed. Geoffrey Sayre-McCord (Ithaca, N.Y.: Cornell University Press, 1988), p. 186, and John McDowell, "Non-Cognitivism and Rule-Following," in *Wittgenstein: To Follow a Rule,* ed. S. Holtzman and C. Leich (London: Routledge & Kegan Paul, 1981), p. 161 fn19. See also Mackie, *Ethics: Inventing Right and Wrong,* p. 100.

34. I could also discuss here the work of David Wiggins, especially "Truth, Invention and the Meaning of Life" (*Proceedings of the British Academy* LXII, 1976), which has been very influential.

35. By "general" I mean to signal that McDowell is not saying that particular instances of value or color depend for their existence on particular hu-

object's being red should be understood (and by and large *is* understood) as its having the disposition to look red to us in appropriate circumstances.[36] Here we have a new account of objectivity. We could correctly call color, on this view, subjective and objective. It is subjective in the sense that it is understood relative to the capacities of subjects. It is objective in the sense that its existence does not depend on reception by any particular subjects. In this sense the independence required for objectivity is preserved. We can make a strong analogy with values. We can understand an object's having value as its having the disposition to produce responses of a certain kind in us in appropriate circumstances.[37] Values can be called subjective and objective with equal correctness, in the same way as colors.

McDowell also wants to deny the strict distinction between cog-

---

man response. By the phrase "do not have to be seen as" I mean to allow, though McDowell does not, that there could be cases of value that are not even coordinate with *general* human dispositions.

36. McDowell, "Values and Secondary Qualities," pp. 110f. This paper originated in a seminar in 1978 with Mackie and R. M. Hare on Mackie's *Ethics: Inventing Right and Wrong.* McDowell thinks that the pre-philosophical view Mackie attributes to "common sense" is incoherent. For it first requires that redness be construed as not essentially phenomenal and then postulates a property in objects themselves that resembles redness as we experience it. But what could the resemblance be, he asks, other than essentially phenomenal (how it looks to us)? McDowell thinks that even with primary qualities it is a mistake to deny that our experience of them is essentially subjective. It is better, he says, to think of the difference between primary and secondary qualities this way: both colors and shapes are properties that things *are represented* as having, but colors are represented as distinctively phenomenal and shapes are not. He quotes Gareth Evans, "Things Without the Mind," in Zak van Straaten, ed., *Philosophical Subjects: Essays Presented to P. F. Strawson* (Oxford: Clarendon Press, 1980), p. 96: "To deny that . . . primary properties are *sensory* is not at all to deny that they are *sensible* or *observable.*"

37. There will be a certain kind of circularity in the account, in which the properties and our responses to them are defined in terms of each other. It is consistent with this to argue, as Wiggins does, that we can have the response before the property is *identified.* See Wiggins, *Needs, Values, Truth: Essays in the Philosophy of Value* (Oxford: Oxford University Press, 1987), p. 198.

nitive capacities like belief and non-cognitive ones like desire, and hence to deny that "pure facts" and values can always in principle be disentangled.[38] The central cases are content-full ("thick") value terms like "gentleman." My nanny, when I was growing up, told me that you could recognize a gentleman by whether he polished the backs of his shoes. Ordinary people polished the fronts, but only gentlemen the backs. Here is a criterion that we can use as a test for an evaluation. McDowell proposes that we can only know how to apply the value concept through such a criterion if we are inside the evaluative framework or the form of life that places value on it.[39] In this case we have to be inside the British class system. Then our confident use of the value concept is natural to us; it becomes "second nature" by enculturation and habit, by what he calls "a decent upbringing."[40] McDowell wants to deny that seeing the value in this

38. McDowell thinks the prescriptivist makes the same kind of mistake as Mackie about the non-evaluative base to which we attribute value when making value judgments. He thinks R. M. Hare tries to preserve objectivity by making the purely factual character of the world independent of how it strikes any evaluators. About the world thus construed as value-free, the prescriptivist (according to McDowell) then supposes we have our desires, which we may express in value judgments; but the purely descriptive elements in such judgments can always in principle be disentangled from the evaluative. See McDowell, "Non-Cognitivism and Rule-Following," pp. 141f.

39. McDowell thinks the prescriptivist is misled by the bogus picture of understanding concepts as having one's mental wheels, as it were, on some independently existing rails. The image is from Wittgenstein, *Philosophical Investigations* 218. McDowell cites, as evidence that R. M. Hare is interested in defending objectivity in this way, chapter 2 of *Freedom and Reason* (Oxford: Clarendon Press, 1963). But Hare is not there trying to defend the objectivity he *is* interested in (which I called earlier "Kantian") by basing it on some other kind of objectivity of pure description. It is true that he believes that the evaluative and descriptive meanings can in principle be disentangled, but it is consistent with this to concede that to learn the descriptive meaning it is necessary to *have been* (but not to *be*) engaged in the form of life that makes just these descriptive features salient. It is possible to grow up in, and then reject, the form of life in which "gentleman" is understood.

40. Naturalistic platonism is to be distinguished from "rampant platon-

kind of case has to be distinguished as a desire rather than a belief, something non-cognitive rather than something cognitive, a state of the will rather than of the intellect. He thinks we should see values as being there in the world, making demands on our reason, but not there in the world independently of our dispositions to be moved by them.[41]

But now we have to face the danger of relativism, and also Mackie's argument from relativity. Mackie thinks there is objective truth in science but not in morals. He sees just too much difference in moral beliefs between societies, historical periods, and different groups and classes within a complex community. Disagreement by itself does not show that there is no objective truth in morals; for there are also radical differences in beliefs about history or biology or cosmology. But Mackie thinks the disagreements in science and the disagreements in morals are differently explained. Disagreement in science results, he says, from speculative inferences or explanatory hypotheses based on inadequate evidence. But disagreement about morals seems to reflect people's participation in different ways of life. Mackie thinks the causal connection is mainly that way round: it is that people approve of monogamy because they participate in a monogamous way of life rather than that they participate in a mo-

---

ism." Naturalistic platonism holds that our confidence that we can "go on the same way" in applying our present concepts (descriptive and evaluative) in new contexts is based on no more, and no less, than our shared forms of life. See McDowell, *Mind and World* (Cambridge, Mass.: Harvard University Press, 1994), p. 91.

41. J. E. J. Altham has the useful term "besire." See "The Legacy of Emotivism" in Graham MacDonald and Crispin Wright, eds., *Fact, Science and Morality: Essays on A. J. Ayer's "Language, Truth and Logic"* (Oxford: Blackwell, 1986), pp. 275-88. McDowell himself uses Moore's term "appreciate" to indicate that the kind of "seeing" he has in mind is a feeling of the force of the value, which is itself a "being moved" in a certain way. See McDowell, "Virtue and Reason," reprinted in *Virtue Ethics*, ed. Roger Crisp and Michael Slote (New York: Oxford University Press, 1997), p. 143 fn4 and p. 144. McDowell does not make the attribution to Moore.

nogamous way of life because they approve of monogamy. He says that the actual variations in moral codes are more readily explained by supposing they reflect different ways of life than by supposing they express perceptions, most of them seriously inadequate and badly distorted, of objective values.

Now McDowell thinks he has a reply to this argument, but I think it fails. He talks, as I said earlier, about second nature, and appeals to Aristotle's view that ethical requirements are there in any case, whether or not we are responsive to them. In this sense the requirements are objective. But McDowell points out that Aristotle is not interested in combating doubts about the specific ethical norms he describes, but "simply takes them for granted."[42] Objectivity, McDowell says, does not require some kind of detachment from cultural influence. All that is necessary to open our eyes to these requirements is a decent upbringing (and, Aristotle would add, the right raw material). But what about the problem that the values that become second nature in one culture (for example, Athens in the fifth century) are different from values embedded in another, or not securely embedded in any culture at all? If second nature is allowed to be culturally variable in this way, then values tied to second nature will be culturally relative and may be corrupt.[43] McDowell's solution is to insist also on the essential contestability of ethics. He acknowledges that values are different from colors this way. We should never be unreflectively content, he says, with the current state of our value

42. McDowell insists that Aristotle cannot be trying to produce a foundation for ethics in human nature, since his account of nature is already permeated with ethics (it is largely an account of "second nature"). See McDowell, *Mind and World*, p. 79. He contrasts himself with MacIntyre in *After Virtue*, whose view of Aristotle he calls "a historical monstrosity" that could arise only after the false but characteristically modern sense of the need for a foundation for ethics in the face of a "disenchanted" nature.

43. The values are correlatively defined with our natural responses, so that, as Wiggins says, "both are made for each other." See David Wiggins, "A Sensible Subjectivism," in *Needs, Values, Truth*, p. 199. But then if the "natural" responses are culturally variable, so are the values.

judgments as an undistorted perception of the relevant aspect of reality.[44] But Aristotle *was* content. As McDowell says, Aristotle simply took the ethical norms for granted. McDowell acknowledges an Aristotelian "smugness" at this point, but he thinks the smugness can easily be corrected for.

It is not so easy, however. Aristotle's failure is systematic. He thinks he has a culturally mediated human universal. But his view of the chief good for human beings includes as components both power over others and prestige, both of them competitive goods (in the sense that they can be possessed by some only if they are not possessed, or are possessed less, by others).[45] It is this, not just his application of the view to women and slaves, that is objectionable to a supporter of altruism or even impartial justice. Aristotle is not wrong to say that we aim at these competitive goods (we *do*), but he is wrong to derive from our naturally aiming at them the conclusion that they are good. He does not make Murdoch's (and Kant's) concession about the corruption of human nature both at the individual level and at the level of the group.[46] In Murdoch's terms, he confuses the fire with the sun. Kant's view was that the influence of other people on a single human being is to make him worse. As he says, "Envy, the lust for power, greed, and the malignant inclinations bound up with these, besiege his nature, contented within itself *as*

---

44. McDowell, "Values and Secondary Qualities," p. 120.

45. I have argued for this in "God's Commands and Moral Realism," forthcoming. Some relevant texts are *Nicomachean Ethics* I, 2, 1094b8-10; IV, 3, 1123b23-24, 1124a5-12, 22-26, 1124b12-15; VI, 5, 1140b8-11; VI, 8, 1141b24; IX, 7, 1168a5-10; X, 7, 1178a1; *Politics* I, 5, 1254a21-23; III, 4, 1277a13-b29.

46. There is a similar difficulty in Sabina Lovibond, *Realism and Imagination in Ethics* (Oxford: Blackwell, 1983). I owe to Ben Lipscomb the point that she starts with the view that our forms of life give us the vocabulary to express moral truth (she is a realist), but she is afraid of the potentially authoritarian implications of this. She wants to tolerate moral deviance and difference of opinion. Nonetheless, she says (p. 204), "It is up to the community concerned to decide when *anomie* has gone too far — when people's behaviour has begun to 'stammer' unacceptably." And this "up to" is normative, not merely descriptive.

soon as he is among human beings."[47] Following this lead, Reinhold Niebuhr suggested that while altruistic love may be possible for individuals in some circumstances, it is not possible for social groups, and that is why he entitled his book *Moral Man and Immoral Society.* Let me give one example. As individuals we citizens of rich countries like the United States find it difficult to lower our standard of living to what impartial justice would require. The normative "common sense" judgments about what is "need" and what is "luxury" are pervasive in the culture and especially in the media. Our "second nature" is in this regard biased towards our own advantage, just as our biological nature is. Go to the mall and watch it. Even if it is possible for an individual to reach moral discomfort with the *status quo,* the culture is a contrary tendency that has to be continually resisted. From the perspective of altruism or impartial justice our nature, including our second nature, is radically liable to endorse what is not good. So second nature does not provide the kind of guide to moral truth that McDowell needs.

The expressivist way to deal with relativity is to insist on the function of value language to express or withhold endorsement. In order to maintain the possibility of the right kind of critical distance from culture, we need to hold out the possibility of refusing to endorse aspects of our familiar context. Earlier I gave the example of "gentleman," a word that sums up a whole class system. This system may have become "second nature," controlling whole swaths of a person's daily life. But if moral thought is to have a critical function, it must be possible for the moral agent to exercise the will in a refusal to submit any longer to this system. He is not disengaging from his culture as a whole, which might well be impossible, a "view from nowhere." But he takes some region of description, and sets himself to eradicating its influence on his value judgment.[48] He wants not to care any longer

47. Kant, *Religion within the Limits of Reason Alone,* VI, 93-94 (emphasis original). The German for "contented within itself" is *an sich genügsame.*

48. R. M. Hare calls this a set of "criteria." It is helpful here to return to Roberts's account of emotion. On that account, we have concerns and then

whether people polish the backs of their shoes. There can be something sad about this change. Certain kinds of pleasure, for example the pleasure in walking round a stately home, may not be available any longer except ambiguously. But because he can refuse to endorse his affective responses, he is not constrained by the logic of the ("thick") value terms to fit himself to the norms of his culture.

On my view an evaluative judgment involves some state like a motivation, or a desire, or a concern (again, we lack a generic term in English), because the function of the judgment is to endorse or withhold endorsement of some such state.[49] An objection is that amoralists (without moral motivation) can nonetheless make moral evaluations.[50] Prescriptivism replies that the "inverted commas"

---

construals of situations on the basis of those concerns. It may be impossible to disentangle experientially the construal present in an emotion and the concern that is taken up into it. What I am insisting on is something different, that it *is* at least in principle possible to disentangle the concern-construal mixture from the endorsement of it. It is easy to confuse these two disentanglings, and to conclude mistakenly that the second is impossible because the first is.

49. This is what David Brink distinguishes as "appraiser internalism" in *Moral Realism and the Foundations of Ethics* (Cambridge: Cambridge University Press, 1989), p. 40. It is not what Michael Smith calls "internalism" in *The Moral Problem* (Oxford: Blackwell, 1994), pp. 60-63.

50. For a discussion of the amoralist objection to expressivism, see David Solomon, "Moral Realism and the Amoralist," *Midwest Studies in Philosophy* XII (Minneapolis: University of Minnesota Press, 1988), pp. 377-93. He argues that the most plausible forms of amoralism (like that of Thrasymachus in the *Republic*) cannot be used by the realist to make this point against the expressivist, because they are themselves inconsistent with moral realism. Thrasymachus thought (though his view is not consistent) that what is true in morality is constituted by the beliefs and actions of the most powerful members of society. But if so, then the moral truth is not independent in the right way for the realist objector. See also Michael Smith, *The Moral Problem*, pp. 68-71. Al Mele uses an argument from what he calls "moral listlessness" in "Internalist Moral Cognitivism and Listlessness," *Ethics* 106 (July 1996): 725-53. Michael Stocker refers to the various kinds of state in which the loss of connection occurs as "depressions" in "Desiring the Bad: An Essay in Moral Psychology," *Journal of Philosophy* (1979): 738-53.

kind of amoralist can say something is good meaning merely "what most people call good," and can call something good in this sense without the corresponding motivation. But the expressivist can allow other kinds. Consider the first realist concession, about the precarious and incomplete character of our moral knowledge. If this concession is right, we are probably in and out of some degree of amoralism on a regular basis. The notion of endorsement I have been pressing acknowledges a magnetic center, in Murdoch's term, and on the agent's side, a sense that there is an "I" who has developed a consistent position to take in normative discussion.[51] Someone who is morally listless has lost the sense of things making sense in this way, both on the "world" side and on the "self" side. The expressivist has a way to understand one thing that is horrible about this kind of experience. The listless person can no longer do endorsement of the kind I have been talking about, and so cannot make evaluative judgments of the full-blooded kind. But the very real possibility of this kind of experience does not show that the expressivist is wrong about what this kind of evaluative judgment requires.

7. New-Wave Realism: David Brink

This chapter started with G. E. Moore's analysis of the naturalistic fallacy.[52] Moore argued that it was fallacious to identify value properties and non-value properties. He thought this followed from showing that the value terms and the non-value terms (natural or supernatural) did not mean the same. His argument for this was that one can always sensibly doubt that goodness is the same as some proposed non-evaluative property, such as pleasure or the disposi-

---

51. See Gibbard, *Wise Choices, Apt Feelings,* p. 75.

52. I could have discussed in this section Richard Boyd, for example his paper "How to Be a Moral Realist," pp. 181-228.

tion to produce pleasure, or being commanded by God. The new-wave argument, for example that of David Brink, is that the failure of property identity does not follow from the failure of meaning identity. The "third realist concession" (R3) is that a value term and a descriptive term that do not mean the same can point to the same causal property.

Brink denies what he calls the semantic test of properties, which is the claim that synonymy is a test of property identity. His move relies on developments in the theory of meaning and reference which I cannot here describe in detail. Putnam's thought experiment about Twin Earth will serve to introduce them.[53] We imagine a world very much like Earth, except that the oceans, lakes, rivers, etc. are filled with a liquid which looks, tastes, etc. like water, and which the local inhabitants call "water," but which is in fact composed not of H_2O but of some other molecular structure XYZ. Putnam argues that we would say that this is *not* water, and necessarily is not; names and natural kind terms are *rigid designators,* designating the same entity in every possible world. When we say, therefore, that water = H_2O, such statements are necessarily true. The property *being water* is identical with the property *being composed of H_2O molecules,* even though the terms "being water" and "being composed of H_2O molecules" are not synonymous. We can add to this account of property identity the "causal" theory of reference, very roughly that names and natural kind terms refer in virtue of an original "dubbing" by speakers in *causal* contact with the referent, who then pass along the ability to refer in virtue of being in causal contact with each other. Applying this to goodness, we can say that we are in causal contact with some property (Brink says it might be natural or supernatural, though he prefers a natural property), and we refer to this by using different terms which

53. See H. Putnam, "The Meaning of 'Meaning,'" in K. Gunderson, ed., *Minnesota Studies in the Philosophy of Science* 7 (Minneapolis: University of Minnesota Press, 1975), pp. 131-93. See also Brink, *Moral Realism and the Foundations of Ethics,* p. 162.

are not synonymous with each other; "goodness" is the evaluative route for picking it out, but our value theory will tell us what the natural or supernatural property is which is identical to this (though picked out by a description, not an evaluation).

It might be helpful to give a simple illustration of the causal connection with the good that this kind of realism proposes.[54] Suppose I am traveling in Italy and I feel thirsty for the familiar, a tall glass of cool milk. But I am in fact, though I do not realize it, dehydrated. Milk will be bad for me, because hard to digest, and *acqua minerale con gaz* would be much better. There is a possible feedback loop in which either I get the milk, feel worse, and next time find myself wanting something different, or I cannot get milk, buy the bottled water, feel much better, and next time find myself preferring the water. In either case, it is natural to think I am being guided by my good (in this case my non-moral good), in a process of largely unreflective experimentation, followed by positive and negative associations and reinforcements.[55]

54. The example is drawn from Peter Railton, "Moral Realism," *Philosophical Review* 95 (1986): 163-207.

55. Other examples are the explanation we find it natural to give of a person's actions in terms of that person's moral character, and the explanation of the growth of antislavery sentiment in the United States from the fact that chattel slavery got worse in the eighteenth and nineteenth centuries. See Nicholas Sturgeon, "Moral Explanations," in *Morality, Reason and Truth,* ed. David Copp and David Zimmerman (Totowa, N.J.: Rowman and Allanheld, 1985), pp. 49-78, especially section III. New-wave realism has a reply here to Mackie's argument from relativism. If these are genuine explanations, then the relevant distinction between morals and science disappears. Mackie started with the radical differences we can observe in moral beliefs, and claimed that, unlike differences in scientific belief, these argued against objective truth in morals. The reason for the difference with science, he thought, was one of explanation; the scientific differences are best explained by inadequate evidence, etc., while the moral differences are best explained by different ways of life. But the tourist story and the other examples suggest that an evaluative property might play a genuinely explanatory role; and if so, the proposed difference with science disappears.

Brink is chiefly interested in defending the identity of goodness with a natural property — roughly, human flourishing and what produces this.[56] I am going to take the supernatural property which Moore considered, that something is commanded by God. This example returns us to Mackie's point that objective prescriptions did make sense when people believed in a divine lawgiver. It is not my purpose at this point to try to be subtle about just what kind of divine command theory I am talking about. I will deal with that in the second chapter, and I will distinguish between the attraction implicit in "good" and the constraint implicit in "command." The question at issue at the moment is whether to accept the proposal, following the new-wave realists, that being good is the same property as being commanded by God, even though "good" and "commanded by God" do not mean the same.[57]

Although I am going to use the third realist concession, I want to insist on a difference between the way the terms "good" and "water" work. I think there is a version of Moore's open question argument that still applies, even after the changes in the philosophy of meaning and reference which I have briefly described. Suppose there is a Twin Earth which differs from ours not in the use of the term "water" but in the use of the term "good."[58] If the inhabitants of

---

56. Brink calls himself an "objective utilitarian." What is important for present purposes, however, is not his normative theory, but his realism.

57. "Right" would be better here than "good," but I am following Moore. See Robert M. Adams, "Divine Command Metaethics Modified Again," *Journal of Religious Ethics* 7, no. 1 (1979); and by William Alston, "Some Suggestions for Divine Command Theorists," from *Christian Theism and the Problems of Philosophy*, ed. Michael Beaty (Notre Dame: Notre Dame Press, 1989).

58. I am relying here on a thought experiment suggested by Terence Horgan and Mark Timmons, "New-Wave Moral Realism Meets Moral Twin Earth," in *Rationality, Morality, and Self-interest*, ed. J. Heil (Lanham, Md.: Rowman & Littlefield, 1993), pp. 115-33. See also Mark Timmons, "On the Epistemic Status of Considered Moral Judgements," *Southern Journal of Philosophy* 29 (Spindel Conference Supplement, 1990): 97-129. For the prescriptivist original, see R. M. Hare, *The Language of Morals*, pp. 148-49.

both worlds use the term to commend, but *what* they commend is very different, I think we would say that an *essential* function of the term is retained, even though the criteria of application are different. The controlling function of a term like "water" is to give the natural kind, not the phenomenal meaning. (Webster gives, as the first definition, "a colorless transparent liquid etc.," but then goes on to give the chemical definition.) But surely we would say that the inhabitants of Moral Twin Earth are using "good" in the *same* way as us, namely to commend, but with different beliefs and theories about what is good. An essential function of "good" is to commend. Within a value judgment, the function is to endorse such a commendation. Genuine dispute between us and the Moral Twin Earthers about the good is therefore possible, whereas dispute about water with the Twin Earthers would be silly, since we would be talking past each other. This does not mean, however, that the divine command theorist cannot use the new-wave strategy after all. The Moral Twin Earth case simply shows us that, unlike in Twin Earth, the underlying structure (e.g., being commanded by God) does not in the case of "good" give us a *sufficient* base for the use of the term, since we also need to know if what is being called good is being commended. When we call something good we are not merely pointing to the causal property but expressing some act or disposition within what I called at the beginning the *orectic* family.

An advance has still been made. The divine command theorist can point to the underlying structure of a thing's being commanded by God, and can claim that many people use the term "good" without understanding this structure. If my earlier account was correct there is a property which the use of the term "good" points to, namely the experienced causal property which Murdoch calls "magnetic"; but using the term "good" in a judgment is not merely pointing to this property, but endorsing the attraction. Consider one of the fallen angels, who knows that something is commanded by God, but does *not* commend it. Indeed it is just because that thing is commanded by God that the fallen angel rejects it.[59] But to say this is quite consistent with saying that there is a necessary structure lying behind what is good, namely that it is commanded by God. We need to distinguish within an evaluative judgment between the experience of the magnetic force and the endorsement of our attraction by it. We can now see that the divine command theorist has a particular account of what this magnetic force is and *towards* what it is an attraction. The divine command theorist holds that we are experiencing what Murdoch describes as a "call" (though Murdoch is deeply suspicious of the picture of a personal God who could give a call). On this theory the force that attracts us is God's call. Even Lucifer experiences this call, but rejects it. When we experience this force as a call *and* endorse our attraction to it, we are judging that the force is a call that deserves our obedience.

It is a merit of this version of divine command theory that it can account for the ways in which theists and non-theists both do and do not use the term "good" (and other value terms) in the same way. They are both using the term for an essential function, which is to commend. Moreover, they are both using the term in a value judgment to endorse an attraction toward something. But the believer identifies what it is that is attracting or pulling her as God's call, and the non-believer does not. In the same way H_2O is what water in fact is, even though the first meaning of the term "water" (according to Webster) is phenomenal, "a colorless, transparent liquid etc." Corresponding to the phenomenal definition of water will be the definition of "good" as "the most general term of commendation." But, unlike the case of "water," this will be (if I am right) an essential

---

59. I think this is the right account of the cryptic saying by Milton's Lucifer, "Evil, be thou my good." Is such an angel no longer using the term "good" properly? The divine command theorist should say that the angel has the wrong criteria, but is still using the term "good" for an essential function, which is to commend. There is a difference in the way Lucifer uses the term "evil" and the term "good." He is expressing his endorsement, by the term "good," of what he believes is by *God's* criteria evil.

function of the term. Our practical lives of drinking, washing, and swimming correspond to our practical lives of advising, approving, and admiring. In both cases, according to the proposal, there is an underlying structure; being H_2O is necessary to something's being water, and being commanded by God is necessary to something's being good. But people can use the terms "water" and "good" without knowing this structure, and many people do. If the believer is right, then the non-believer will in fact be picking out this causal property when she correctly calls something good, even though this is not at all her intention. However, because of the fragility of our value knowledge conceded in the first realist concession, even the believer has to admit that she might be wrong in naming the pull in some case as God's call. This is not to say that she has to be tentative in this naming, or lukewarm in her commitment to obey. But she has to concede that opting for obedience here is epistemologically risky. She might be wrong.

Does the insistence on the commendatory function of "good" mean that the good is there only when someone is commending? Should we take this to mean that the good is projected and so created by the evaluator? I have argued before that we should not take the point this way. The divine command theorist could finesse the difficulty, by saying that the good *is* always being commended by someone, namely God. But I think the projectivist line is a mistake even for the divine command theorist. When we commend, we should say, we are not putting something into the world that was not there before. Not even God is doing that in evaluating, though God is doing this in creating what God then evaluates. Rather, we are responding to something that is already there, and it is a felt causal force that we are responding to, though perhaps here there is a disanalogy to how an impassible God evaluates. God, we are told, sees that the created world is good, but I do not myself understand how to fit this into a doctrine that God's intuition is intellectual and thus productive (to put it in Kantian terms). Fortunately this is not the topic of this chapter or this book. The structure which we respond to, and which we may experience as a call deserving submission, is there whether we experience it or not. But to say that the structure would be *good* whether commended or not is, if we read it one way, a mistake in philosophical grammar. It does not make sense to say that something is good that is not evaluated as good. It is tempting to reply that something can be good in the sense that it is *fit* to be commended, even if it is not yet commended; by the color analogy, something can be red in the sense that it is disposed to cause the sensation of red in certain circumstances, whether it is actually causing this or not. But this is just where the color analogy breaks down. To say that something is *fit* to be commended is already to commend it. "Fit" is a term of evaluation (even if I say, "His dirty T-shirt fits his dirty jeans"). But to say that something is disposed to cause the sensation of red is not already to say that it is causing it.

8. Norm-Expressivism: Allan Gibbard

Allan Gibbard denies the new-wave realist claim that value properties have causal effects on the world.[60] Nonetheless, he does think that a causal process operates in the world to produce our affective response mechanisms, and this causal process results in our good. This is what I will call "the third expressivist concession" (E3). He thinks that the moral emotions such as guilt and resentment are themselves the fruit of a beneficent causal process; though the process is not benevolent because it is not personal (it is evolutionary). The emotions are good for us because they enable coordination,

---

60. He thinks the postulation of such a causal role is gratuitous. In the case of physical science, we can say that no full explanation of why physicists have the beliefs they do about atoms etc. can avoid citing facts about those entities. But he agrees with Mackie that no corresponding realm of normative facts needs to appear in a full explanation of why we have the normative beliefs we do. See Gibbard, *Wise Choices, Apt Feelings,* p. 122.

broadly conceived.[61] His view is that evolution, working on the hunter-gatherer social groupings that prevailed for most of human existence, selected in favor of affective dispositions in us which promote coordination, and hence the human goods that are only available through coordination. In particular, evolution gave us specifically human kinds of anger such as outrage and resentment, and it gave us the feeling of guilt, which is an adaptive response to anger because it invites reconciliation, and thus promotes cooperation instead of conflict between the parties. While the propensities to these emotions (and others, such as shame and moral inspiration) may have very different manifestations in different kinds of societies, Gibbard thinks there are common patterns here that suggest an evolutionary origin. He is not saying that the overall goodness of these patterns *follows* from their evolutionary origin. He allows that in our present environment evolution may have given us affective dispositions that are harmful to us. Nonetheless, in the case of the emotions I mentioned he thinks that it is good for us that we have them. This is the first kind of causal process he discusses, the process by which we have been given through the emotions a route to coordination. A second kind of causal process connects these emotions to the stimuli to which they are responses. Gibbard pictures emotions in one of two ways. They might be physical states of the organism, genetically determined, which stand behind an adaptive syndrome of typical overt responses to external stimuli. Such a syndrome might be the dog barking at an intruder. This picture fits best the emotions of animals, and those human emotions that seem to be culturally invariable (like fear in the presence of a large hostile carnivorous animal). Or, on the second picture, the emotions are self-attributional, and require the agent's conceptualization (drawing on the repertoire of her culture). But on this second picture, as well as the first, emotion is seen as a response to a stimulus, though mediated this time by particular cultural concepts.

61. Gibbard, *Wise Choices, Apt Feelings,* p. 26.

The connection he sees between these emotions and moral judgment is as follows. He wants to find an account of practical rationality in a broad sense, which will give us the kind of objectivity we want. He proposes that to call an act or a feeling "rational" is to endorse it in a broad (or "flavorless") sense, which is roughly to say that the act or feeling "makes sense." This kind of endorsement is the special element that makes normative thought and language normative, and Gibbard insists that no merely descriptive account can get normativity right. To say that something makes sense is to express one's acceptance of norms that permit it. For an agent to judge that her action is morally reprehensible, he says, is for her to express her acceptance of norms that impartially prescribe, for such a situation, guilt on the part of the agent and resentment (or anger) on the part of others.[62]

There is an important truth here that prescriptive realism can incorporate. The truth is that a value judgment endorses not just the particular response but the whole causal network of typical situation and emotional response to the situation invoked by the evaluative term. For an agent to judge that eating prisoners is wrong, to return one last time to this example, is for her to accept the norm that prescribes guilt on the part of the eater and anger on the part of the rest of us. She is expressing her acceptance of the whole structure in which she is embedded, in which people respond in this way to this kind of action. What Gibbard has added is the widening of the scope of the evaluation to include this whole structure. In this section I am going to do something different from Gibbard, but faithful to the concession as just formulated. I am going to give a Kant-

---

62. For some difficulties see John E. Hare, *The Moral Gap,* pp. 182-88. For example, it is a difficulty that guilt seems to be the second kind of emotion he distinguishes, the kind that is mediated by particular cultural concepts, in this case especially those of the great monotheistic religions. For this means that an evolutionary account should explain why we have these particular cultural concepts. See also Justin D'Arms and Daniel Jacobson in "Expressivism, Morality, and the Emotions," *Ethics* 104 (July 1994): 739-63.

style argument for what I will call a "postulate of prudence," that an agent has to assume that the world is such that her evaluation of something as good to pursue is consistent with her happiness. The connection with Gibbard is that he uses evolution as a substitute for or improvement on the doctrine of providence; but the realist implications are the same in either case, whether evolution turns out to have the required explanatory power or not. The argument for the postulate of prudence will have the same form as the argument for the moral postulate of a providential ordering, which I gave at some length in chapter three of *The Moral Gap*. The difference is that in the moral case, the agent's postulate was of a system in which virtue is rewarded by happiness, while in the present case her postulate is merely of the consistency of her evaluation with her happiness.[63]

The argument for the postulate of prudence proceeds by pointing out how many assumptions are required by an evaluation of something as good to pursue. I will mention five, but this is not supposed to be an exhaustive list. I will put the five in terms of goods pursued, but the point could be made more widely about our affective lives in general. (1) First, I have to assume that the good I pursue can be achieved. To see that this is so, imagine a demon like the one Descartes imagines in the *Meditations*. But this demon is not inter-

---

63. The postulates are, however, related in two ways. First, the postulate of prudence is one of the requirements for the moral postulate. If happiness is not possible, then the highest good for morality is not possible either. As Mill says, "If (we know) no happiness is to be had at all by human beings, the attainment of it cannot be the end of morality or of any rational conduct" (*Utilitarianism,* chapter 2). This first connection means that it is appropriate to start with the fact that we are under the moral law (what Kant called "the fact of reason") as the basis for the need for a postulate of prudence, just as the moral argument starts from this same fact as the basis for the moral postulate. The second connection is that if we assume that the desire to be a morally good person is one of the desires that most people have (though it may be in some people a relatively weak desire), then happiness requires that this desire be achievable consistently with our other desires. But the consistency of virtue and happiness is what the moral postulate is designed to secure.

ested, like the Cartesian one, in mucking up my epistemic life but my pursuit of happiness. Whenever, then, I try to achieve some good, the demon arranges that I produce something bad. In such a situation, I would stop trying to achieve good. There would be no point to the effort. So there is an assumption here about the world and my relation to it. My emotions and desires have to be coordinated with the way the world is such that my basic concerns fit at least roughly what the world allows. (2) Second, I have to assume that the good I aim at is possible *as a result* of my effort. It is not enough, for example, that it would happen anyway, whether I tried to produce it or not. Again, this is because if my effort is not required, it loses its point. (3) Third, I have to assume that I can will my good not merely at the moment but consistently. This is not a trivial assumption, given how many competing goods I may be minded to pursue. Many of the goods I am likely to pursue have both future-directed and con-temporaneous side-constraints. For example, when I set out to purchase a durable good, I have to assume that I am going to continue enjoying it. That is a *future*-directed constraint. I also have to assume that there is not something else I *now* want more to do or to get with the same money. This brings up the key assumption, (4), that the goods I pursue are at least by and large consistent with each other. At the moment I take the chocolate eclair, do I believe it is consistent with my losing the weight I have planned to lose? No, but this sort of case is notoriously hard to explain. It is indeed a requirement of a good account of the practical life that it should *make* this kind of weakness of the will hard to explain, because we experience it as mysterious and any account that makes it straightforward is almost certainly misdescribing it. Perhaps something like Aristotle's account is right (though the interpretation of Aristotle here is much disputed).[64] During the episode of weakness the factual premise of the

---

64. Aristotle, *Nicomachean Ethics* VII, 3, 1146b30ff. See what Norman O. Dahl calls "the traditional interpretation," *Practical Reason, Aristotle, and Weakness of the Will* (Minneapolis: University of Minnesota Press, 1984), pp. 139-55.

virtuous syllogism is weakened by the presence of the contrary desire, so that it is only half-known. Because of my desire for the eclair, I only half-know that it has 500 calories and will destroy my calorie target for the whole weekend. And because of this weakening in the virtuous syllogism, the vicious syllogism is triumphant. In any case, my claim is that in the normal non-acratic case we assume that the goods we pursue on some occasion are consistent with at least the central goods we pursue in our lives as a whole. (5) I have to make assumptions about other people, that what they evaluate as good to pursue is at least roughly consistent with what I evaluate as good to pursue. This is because so many of the goods I am likely to pursue depend for their achievement on the cooperation of others. In order to get on with ordinary life I have to make charitable assumptions about the drivers of other cars and the check-out cashiers at supermarkets. In addition, as a philosopher, I have to make assumptions about the good will and truth-seeking objectivity of the audiences for my books. When I add these five assumptions together, and suppose the world is such that they are all justified, then I will also have postulated, when I evaluate something as good to pursue, that this evaluation and pursuit is consistent with my happiness.

Now as with the argument for the moral postulate the difficulty comes with an apparent contradiction in experience. In the case of the moral postulate we do *not* have the experience of an exact proportioning of virtue and happiness. We see virtuous people who are apparently unhappy and vicious people who are apparently happy. Moreover, we do not know of any causation which could bring about the proportioning that practical reason seems to require. This is what produces the need for the postulation of a causation outside our knowledge. Similarly with the postulate of prudence. We do not know of any causation (either internal or external to human agency) that could justify these various assumptions, but we have to postulate that there is one, and that the world is governed by it. We have to assume, for example, that there is no demon to muck up our practical lives. We have to assume that the moral goods we pursue as constituents of our own happiness are at least roughly consistent with our other central goals. (Whether this means that they cease to be moral goods is a question I am not going to discuss.) I think we tend to have two opposite reactions, when the need for the postulate of prudence is pointed out. The first is that, of course, the world and we ourselves are just such that this kind of fit obtains. Only a philosopher would try to make this seem remarkable. But the second is that of course the world and we ourselves are *not* this way. There is constant and obvious lack of fit. Common proverbs are full of the gloomy wisdom, to put it colloquially, that shit happens, that the good die young, that he who has the gold makes the rules. Bernard Williams points to what he thinks is the ancient Greek sense of tragedy, that the world is quite likely not well adjusted to human aspirations.[65] In the face of the ever-present possibility of this outlook, we need a kind of realist faith, that the world and we ourselves in it are in fact governed in such a way that these five assumptions I have mentioned are legitimate, and our pursuing some good is consistent with our happiness. We can then interpret the hints of fit we get as signs of the truth of a larger picture in which the good is, so to speak, more fundamental than the evil. There is no inconsistency between such a faith, realist though it be, and expressivism as I have defended it. What expressivism adds is that in an evaluative judgment I have to put that faith into practice in my decision about when to endorse and when to withhold endorsement.

9. Prescriptive Realism

I want to finish by laying out prescriptive realism as it connects with the concessions I have listed as E1-3 and R1-3. I will return to the example of Peter and Sue which I gave in the introduction. Peter judges

65. Bernard Williams, *Shame and Necessity* (Berkeley: University of California Press, 1994), pp. 163-64.

that the relationship with Sue is worth saving and that this is what God wants from him. The judgment is not merely a report that he feels pulled towards reconciliation, but it expresses his acceptance of norms that prescribe that kind of response to his situation. He is judging that the situation deserves this kind of response. There are three elements here: first, the initial construal of his situation as calling for reconciliation; next, the concern (for Sue, for the relationship, and for faithfulness in relationships) that is taken up into the construal; and then the endorsement of the construal in his judgment. He is claiming in this judgment a Kantian kind of objectivity (E1). He is judging that people like him should respond to this kind of situation in this kind of way. He is also attending to the situation in a way that involves self-discipline, an "unselfing," since his natural inclinations tend towards giving up (R1). In making the judgment he is also claiming objectivity in a different sense, claiming that he is responding to a pull by the relationship that is really there outside his present imperfect attempts at evaluation (E2). But this pull is not independent of him in the sense that it would be there whether *he* is there or not. This kind of pull is from relationships in which humans are embedded, and would not be there without them (R2). He judges that God wants him to be reconciled with Sue, and here he identifies the pull as God's call. This is a causal claim, but he can say that reconciliation would be *good* without identifying this cause (R3). Suppose Sue is not a religious believer. Peter and Sue can still agree that reconciliation would be good, even though Peter will identify God's call here and Sue will not. Prescriptive realism is not itself committed to theism. Finally, when Peter endorses the feeling of pull, he is endorsing not just his feeling on this particular occasion, but the whole set of norms that prescribe this kind of response (E3). In saying that God wants him to be reconciled, he is not merely claiming to report God's mind, but claiming to be part of a structure that he accepts, a structure in which God calls people to the same kind of faithfulness that God has, and in which living that way is consistent with their happiness.

47

God's call comes to Peter, I am supposing, through the pull of the relationship with Sue. In the same way magnetic force can come to an iron ring through other iron rings that are attracted to the original magnet. This is Plato's image (*Ion* 536a): "Well, do you not see that the spectator is the last of the rings I spoke of, which receive their force from one another by virtue of the magnet? . . . But it is the deity who, through all the series, draws the spirit of men wherever he desires, transmitting the attractive force from one into another." So there are three levels of the analysis: first, the cosmic, where we talk about the call; next the level of the human species or the community, of nature or second nature, where we talk about the kind of felt response the norms prescribe; and last the individual, where we talk about the initial response and the endorsement by the agent himself, the endorsement not only of the particular attraction but of the whole structure in which people are attracted in this way. I hope to have shown that this three-level analysis also gives us promising conceptual space for an account of God's authority in human morality. Roughly, we can say that God created us with an emotional and affective make-up, such that we feel the pull of God's call. But value judgment is more than just feeling such a response; it requires us to endorse or to refuse to endorse this response. Unfortunately we are now in a condition in which the response, both immediate and reflective, is skewed by self-preference. Having identified the source of the pull towards the good, however, as God's call, we are now in a more promising position to identify when it is in fact operative. I shall return to this in the second chapter.

Chapter Two

GOD'S COMMANDS

1. Scotus and Calvin

In this chapter I am going to defend a version of divine command theory as the account of the authority of morality which best fits the meta-ethical theory about moral realism and expressivism outlined in the first chapter. Divine command theory, as I shall defend it, is the theory that what makes something obligatory for us is that God commands it. In the first chapter I proposed that an evaluative judgment endorses a response to a pull of the good which is there independently of the evaluation. I also suggested that we can identify this pull of the good as God's call to us. Divine command theory fits what I said in the first chapter, because it sees our obligations as an expression of God's will, and then our judgments of obligation as an expression of our will to recapitulate God's willing in ours. The move from the good to the obligatory, or from attraction to constraint, comes because after the Fall our perception of the good is splintered and disordered. We need to be held back from some of our pursuits, and we need to trust that this constraint is consistent with our good. Divine command theory is an option that most recent ethicists in philosophy have dismissed. Natural law theory has taken possession of the field as the theist alternative to a secular ethical theory. I think this is partly because of the negative power of an argument by Kant, which I am going to respond to in chapter three. But partly it is because ethicists have not taken seriously the complex and difficult writing on this issue by the thirteenth-century Franciscan philosopher and theologian John Duns Scotus.

I am going to proceed by describing and modifying his account, which I think is the best version we have of a divine command theory. I think this project is especially promising for Calvinists, because of the connection between Scotus and Calvin. This connection is both thematic and historical. Calvin is closer, I think, to Scotus than to Thomas Aquinas. This is not surprising, since Scotus was in general more influential than Aquinas in the two hundred years after Scotus's death. It was not until the Counter-Reformation that Thomism assumed its pre-eminence in Roman Catholic thinking. But more particularly, Calvin attended the Collège de Montaigu in Paris, where he did his preliminary work in philosophy, and Montaigu emphasized the Franciscan philosophers. John Major (who was born twenty-five miles from Scotus, but about two hundred years later) was its pre-eminent teacher, and was himself deeply influenced by Scotus and knowledgeable about him.[1] As I proceed I will point out themes in Scotus about the centrality of the will or the heart, and the insistence on divine sovereignty, which are reminiscent of Calvin.[2] Calvin and Scotus share a fundamental distrust of

1. The thesis of a strong influence on Calvin from John Major was stated by Francois Wendel in *Calvin*, trans. Philip Mairet (New York: Harper and Row, 1950), and fully worked out by Karl Reuter, in *Das Grundverstaendnis der Theologie Calvins* (Neukirchen-Vluyn: Neukirchener-Verlag, 1963). An enthusiastic advocate is Thomas F. Torrance, in *The Hermeneutics of John Calvin* (Edinburgh: Scottish Academic Press, 1988), and also Alexander Broadie, *The Shadow of Scotus* (Edinburgh: T. & T. Clark, 1995). A more skeptical reading of the evidence can be found in A. Ganoczy, "Le jeune Calvin: Genèse et évolution de sa vocation réformatrice" (Wiesbaden: F. Steiner, 1966), and A. N. S. Lane, "Calvin's Use of the Fathers and the Medievals," *Calvin Theological Journal* 16 (1981): 149-205.

2. There are also differences, though what looks like a conspicuous one turns out not to be on closer inspection. I refer to Calvin's dislike of the distinc-

attempts to limit by human reason what God can and cannot will. I was delighted to read in Dewey Hoitenga's recent book about Calvin's view of the will that he thinks Calvinists ought to be Scotists.[3] In terms of divine command theory, compare these two quotations, one from Scotus and one from Calvin. Scotus says, "The divine will is the cause of the good, and so a thing is good precisely in virtue of the fact that God wills it."[4] Calvin says, "God's will is so much the highest rule of righteousness that whatever he wills, by the very fact that he wills it, must be considered righteous."[5]

I do not want to take this claim of influence too far, however. Calvin shared with many of his contemporaries an impatience with what he calls the "minutiae" (the tiny details) of the scholastics. Scotus especially is likely to cause this kind of impatience. He has the honorific title of "the subtle doctor," but during the sixteenth century (I quote from the OED under "Dunce"), "the [Scotist] system was attacked with ridicule, first by the humanists, and then by the reformers, as a farrago of needless entities, and useless distinctions. The *Dunsmen* or *Dunses*, on their side, railed against the 'new learning,' and the name *Duns* or *Dunce*, already synonymous with 'cavilling sophist' or 'hairsplitter,' soon passed into the sense of 'dull obstinate person impervious to the new learning,' and of 'blockhead incapable of learning or scholarship.'" My own view is that many of these entities and distinctions are pure gold. The loss of them in philosophical theology now has to be repaired by a painstaking recovery of the tradition and then a new evaluation of its usefulness in our current context. But I have to

---

tion between absolute and ordained power. He does not attribute this to Scotus, and in fact the view he is attacking is not Scotus's view. See David C. Steinmetz, "Calvin and the Absolute Power of God," *Journal of Medieval and Renaissance Studies* 18, no. 1 (Spring 1988): 65-79, and Susan E. Schreiner, "Exegesis and Double Justice in Calvin's Sermons on Job," *Church History* 58 (1989): 322-38.

3. Dewey J. Hoitenga, Jr., *John Calvin and the Will* (Grand Rapids: Baker, 1997), pp. 34-39, 65-67, and 127.

4. *Rep.* 1.48. q.u.

5. *Inst.* 3.22.2.

concede that the subtle doctor's thought is difficult to follow (partly because we do not yet have a definitive text to work from), and I hope the reader of this chapter will persevere and will find the eventual fruit worth the effort. I also do not want to suggest that Scotism is of interest *only* to Calvinists. I think the version of divine command theory which Scotus gives us is the best we have, and anyone should be interested in it who wants to say that what makes something obligatory for us is that God commands it.

2. Why Should I Be Moral?

We can raise the question for a moral agent, "Why should I be moral?", where this is understood not as a prudential question ("Why is morality in my interest?"), but a question about justification, all things considered: "Why should I accept the moral demand as a demand upon *me*?"[6] This is a natural question, one I find myself asking from time to time. I am lying in bed, considering the fact that it is my duty to get up and grade some student papers, and I ask myself, "Why *should* I?" An answer to this question will give the source of normativity. The divine command theorist can say, "because God tells me to." This is going to be helpful if I care about what God tells me to do. What we are going to find in Scotus is an essentially relational account of this divine commanding. Scotus thinks that our final end is to be co-lovers with God, in Latin *condiligentes*. And he thinks that God chooses the route to this end, and gives it to us by command. But the final end is not obedience to the command, but the kind of union of will that we call love. We can follow a bit further the image of the magnet. The magnetic force is transmitted to us through the objects and people and situations that God is choosing

6. See Christine Korsgaard (*The Sources of Normativity* [Cambridge: Cambridge University Press, 1996]), who discusses both what she calls "the normative question" and the failures of attempts to say we do not need an answer.

as our route. At the end of the first chapter I quoted Plato's *Ion* (536a): "Well, do you see that the spectator is the last of the rings I spoke of, which receive their force from one another by virtue of the magnet. . . . But it is the deity who, through all the series, draws the spirit of men wherever he desires, transmitting the attractive force from one into another." On the version of divine command theory I am promoting, the end towards which we are headed is some kind of loving union with God. Using the term "command" to describe what gives the route to this end is traditional, but less appropriate than some such term as "call"; for "command" stresses the power relation rather than the love relation which governs not just the destination but the selection of route.

There are alternative answers to the question "Why should I be moral?"; I will mention just four. This is not supposed to be a complete list, and I am not going to discuss them thoroughly. One is that *reason* demands it. Kant thought that it was the nature of reason to will universal law, and it demands this not only in theoretical thinking about science (for example) but in practical thinking about what to do. He also thought he could base morality on this. But this is one place where I think his argument fails. I cannot go into all the details here. But I think morality is not in fact exclusively universal. I think there are particular moral relations to particular people that do not just generate obligations that anyone would have to anyone else in this sort of situation. Moreover, there are universal laws which eliminate reference to the agent in the way Kant requires, but which would be immoral to will. One example is the Nazis' prescription of ideal Aryan purity.[7]

Another answer we might propose is that the source of the

7. See Allan Gibbard, "Hare's Analysis of 'Ought' and Its Implications," in *Hare and Critics,* ed. Douglas Seanor and N. Fotion (Oxford: Clarendon Press, 1988), pp. 57-72. Christine Korsgaard's view belongs in this category, because she thinks she can derive morality from the nature of reflection. Another variant of this same approach is to found ethics, as Habermas does, on the transcendental conditions of discourse.

moral obligation is the *community* we belong to. We have grown up in a community that respects the moral law, and our identity as agents is at least in part formed by that community. Socrates says that the city is like a parent; it has made us what we are.[8] Perhaps to be true to ourselves, therefore, we have to acknowledge the authority of the moral demand our community instilled into us. The problem with this is that it is relativistic, as I discussed in the previous chapter. I grew up in a community that was socially stratified by class. My family on my mother's side has lived in the same enormous house for hundreds of years. But I have become increasingly uneasy with this stratification. It does not follow from the fact that I grew up a certain way, that I am obliged to continue that way. The community does not have that sort of authority.

A third suggestion is that we can locate the authority of morality in human *nature,* and in particular in the natural human inclinations. Perhaps we can say that we can tell what is good by looking at what we are naturally inclined towards. Henry Veatch says of the chief good, "It is just this end that all men *do* strive for and that is consequently the source of their *true* happiness and satisfaction."[9] There are many versions of natural law theory, but they belong in the present category only if they hold that the moral precepts can be *deduced* from true statements about human nature.[10] Also in this category belong "objective list" utilitarian accounts like James Grif-

8. Michael Sandel, for example, claims that membership in a community can "reach beyond our values and sentiments to engage our identity itself." See *Liberalism and the Limits of Justice* (Cambridge: Cambridge University Press, 1982), p. 153.

9. Henry Veatch, *Aristotle: A Contemporary Appreciation* (Bloomington: Indiana University Press, 1974).

10. Alasdair MacIntyre, *After Virtue* (Notre Dame: University of Notre Dame Press, 1981), p. 52. See also Anthony J. Lisska, *Aquinas's Theory of Natural Law* (Oxford: Clarendon Press, 1996), p. 199, though he denies he is a "deductivist." But not all natural law theorists are deductivist in this way. See John Finnis, *Natural Law and Natural Rights* (Oxford: Oxford University Press, 1980), pp. 33f. In particular, Scotus has a natural law account which is not.

fin's.[11] The problem with this approach will be clear from the first chapter. In Iris Murdoch's terms (drawn from Plato's allegory of the cave in the *Republic*), it confuses the fire and the sun (that is, we confuse what we aim at with what is in fact good). In Calvinist terms, it does not take seriously enough the Fall. It is instructive, as I said in the first chapter, to look at the way Aristotle worked out his teleology. It turns out that for him both power and prestige are components of the human good. He is not wrong, I think, to perceive that we naturally aim at these things; but he is wrong to argue that because we aim at them, they are components of our good.

Finally (though there are other possibilities I am not mentioning) we might say that it is simply *self-evident* that morality is authoritative. In the last chapter G. E. Moore was my example of someone who took such a view. Perhaps morality is like perception. It is self-evident, we might say, when I see a goldfinch in good light, that I am justified in believing that there is a goldfinch there. I have no objection to the notion of perceptual beliefs like this being properly basic. If everything had to be justified, then it would turn out that nothing could be. We do have to start somewhere, and perception seems like a good place. But the problem with this answer is that it is no help in those cases where an agent does not feel the force of the moral demand. Morality is unlike perception this way. I do not have the experience of waking up in the morning and just not trusting my senses. But I do have the experience of simply not feeling the authority of the moral demand; I turn over and go back to sleep.

3. The Affection for Justice
and the Affection for Advantage

To understand Scotus's version of divine command theory, we need to start with his doctrine of the two affections. He takes from

11. James Griffin, *Well-Being* (Oxford: Clarendon Press, 1986), e.g., p. 114.

Anselm (and before him from Augustine) the idea that humans have in their will two basic affections (or intellectual appetites), what he calls the affection for advantage *(affectio commodi)* and the affection for justice *(affectio justitiae)*.[12] All acts of the will, on this view, stem from one affection or the other. The affection for advantage is a natural appetite, an inclination or tendency towards one's own proper perfection or happiness. The affection for justice is the inclination towards intrinsic goods for their own sake (because justice, in the classical conception, gives to each thing what is its due).[13] Take, for example, my delivery in October 1999 of the lectures on which this book is based. I might have been focused on the subject matter for

12. Scotus ties the affection for justice to *amor amicitiae,* love of the friendship-type, which is "on account of the thing willed," and the affection for advantage to *amor concupiscentiae,* love of the desire-type, which is "on account of the one who wills" (*Ord.* 4.49.5). It is not quite right to say that only *amor concupiscentiae* is directed towards the self. Scotus can talk about the devil's inordinate friendship for himself (*Ord.* 2.6.2/4). But the distinction is that the *amor concupiscentiae* (and the affection for advantage) loves something for the sake of the self as an end extrinsic to it. (For comparison, see Aquinas, ST I-IIae, q.26, a.4.) The devil can have friendship for himself; but if he loves God not for God's good but his own, this is the affection for advantage. There are difficult borderline cases, where something is pursued wrongly, but not for one's own sake (where one steals something for a friend, for example). These are difficult because Scotus's principle is that no sinful act is chosen according to the affection for justice, which should mean that these cases have to come under the affection for advantage. I think the best thing to say here is that Scotus has oversimplified (as Kant does in the same context). Thomas Williams discusses this difficulty in "How Scotus Separates Morality from Happiness," *American Catholic Philosophical Quarterly* 49, no. 3 (1995): 425-45. He prefers to adapt the account of the affection for advantage, by translating *in ordine ad se* as "with reference to one's own *nature.*" But this seems to me *ad hoc,* and it is better just to leave these cases as requiring a refinement which Scotus does not provide.

13. See Augustine's *City of God* XI.16: "Rational consideration decides on the position of each thing in the scale of importance, on its own merits, whereas need thinks in terms of means to ends *(quid propter quid expetat).*" Scotus talks of justice as paying what is owed at *Ord.* IV, dist. 46, q.1.

its own sake, *attending* to it as Iris Murdoch says, or I might have been focused psychologically on myself delivering the lectures to the audience and the audience's response to me. Both affections are responses to the pull toward the good. But there is in every person a ranking of the two, and if the affection for advantage is ranked first it will become an *improper* regard for the self. The will of free creatures is, for Scotus, a self-determining power to choose in opposite directions, and this determines whether the free agent acts in accordance with the affection for advantage or the affection for justice. But it has this freedom only because it has the affection for justice. If a creature had only the affection for advantage, it would pursue this by nature but not in freedom. The two affections can have the same objects, even God. For union with God is indeed the proper perfection or happiness of a human agent, and so humans are naturally moved towards it. But this movement is not, Scotus says, a movement towards God for God's own sake, but for the sake of the agent. Scotus is not condemning the affection for advantage. He thinks that we were created to have it. Unfortunately, however, we are born after the Fall with an *inordinate* affection for advantage. We are born with the inclination towards our own advantage *above everything else.* This ranking of the two affections is sinful, and has to be reversed. But this does not mean that the affection for advantage is eliminated. Scotus says of the good in heaven that they "neither were able, nor wished, to dislike having happiness, or to have no desire for it. But they did not want it *more than they wanted God to have* everything good."[14]

14. *Ord.* II, dist. 6, q.2, AW 301 (emphasis added). I will cite the reference in Scotus and the reference to the English translation by Allan Wolter in *Duns Scotus on the Will and Morality* (Washington, D.C.: The Catholic University of America Press, 1997). The passage continues: "Rather they wished for happiness less than they wished God well, for they could moderate their desire for happiness through their liberty." I am grateful to Linda Zagzebski for helping me see, in the need for a new ranking of the two affections, the source of morality as obligation and not merely as attraction.

This passage comes in a detailed analysis of Lucifer's fall, drawn again from Anselm *(The Fall of the Devil)* and behind Anselm, from Augustine.[15] The problem is to explain how the angel could have chosen evil, when he was in the open presence of so much good. Scotus answers that Lucifer first coveted happiness immoderately, and this came from an affection for advantage. It must have done so because every act chosen by the will stems from an affection for justice or for advantage or from some combination of the two, and no sin proceeds from an affection for justice. So Lucifer first sinned "by loving something excessively as his supreme delight." This sinning requires that he also had the affection for justice. Scotus refers to Anselm's thought experiment, in which an angel is imagined who has the affection for advantage and *not* the affection for justice, and so is not free. Such an angel, Scotus says, would be drawn inevitably to what is beneficial, and would covet it above all; but this would not strictly be "willing" at all and would not be imputed to it as sin, because it would have no countervailing affection for justice to restrain it. But Lucifer could sin and did, by wanting happiness as good for himself, rather than loving the good as a good in itself, even though he had the affection for justice that would have made this love of the good in itself possible for him.[16]

Lucifer took something good by nature, his own perfection or happiness, and willed it wrongly (morally badly), with the wrong ranking of the two affections. But it is also possible for free beings to will these natural goods rightly (morally well, as presumably the

15. See Augustine's *De Vera Religione* 13.26, 48.93, where the fallen angels are said to have "loved self more than God," as opposed to "loving God more than self," and where "this is perfect justice, to love the greater objects more and the lesser less."

16. See Augustine, *On Free Will* II, 18, 53: "The will turns to its own private good." Scotus also refers to Augustine's statement that this is the supreme perversity of the will, which is to use as means what is to be enjoyed as an end, and treat as an end what is to be used as a means. Augustine, *Eighty-three Different Questions*, q.30.

archangel Michael does). One way to do this is to will them without essential orientation towards the self, as for example when an agent wills some natural good for someone else for that other person's own sake. If we accept that God is the end or goal to which everything is headed, it is possible to love that end either *as* one's own end or *as* the end of all. There is an extreme way to put this difference between the two kinds of love. We can imagine that there was a choice, which in fact there never is, between God's good and ours. If we had only the love for God *as* our good, we could not say, with Luther, and with generations of Presbyterian ministers at their ordination, "I happily submit to damnation for the sake of the glory of God." How could Luther say such a thing? He is commenting on Paul's exclamation, "For I could wish that I myself were accursed and cut off from Christ for the sake of my own people."[17] Calvin interprets the passage as Luther does, though less exuberantly, but he recognizes that for Paul "it was that his mind being overwhelmed, he burst forth into this extreme wish." The point is not that this extreme choice is one we would ever have to face. But it makes the point vividly that we do frequently have to make the choice between putting first either ourselves or the glory of God.

4. Moral Goodness

We can now discuss how Scotus sees the relation between morality and nature. He describes the connection between moral and natural good in the following difficult passage, which I will call "the moral goodness passage": "The moral goodness of an act consists in its having all that the agent's right reason declares must pertain to the act or the agent in acting. This description is explained as follows:

17. Romans 9:3. Another relevant text is Matthew 27:45, where Jesus seems to be willing to take separation from his father as the price for our salvation. Moses, too, offers for the sake of the people to be blotted out of God's book; see Exodus 32:32.

Just as the primary goodness of a being, called 'essential' and consisting in the integrity and perfection of the being itself, implies positively that there is no imperfection, so that all lack or diminution of perfection is excluded, so the being's secondary goodness, which is something over and above *(superveniens)* or 'accidental,' consists in its being perfectly suited to or in complete harmony with something else — something which ought to have it or which it ought to have."[18]

To understand the various distinctions in this passage, we need to see the background in Aristotle. There is a kind of goodness, which Scotus here calls "primary" goodness, which a substance has when it lacks nothing that is necessary to its being the substance it is.[19] Every substance has this kind of being and this kind of goodness. An armadillo must have, if it exists, all that is necessary to being an armadillo; and if it has this, it is to that extent good. This kind of goodness needs to be distinguished from another kind, which Scotus calls "secondary" goodness. This is important for our present purposes because it is going to turn out that moral goodness is a kind of secondary goodness. Secondary goodness is *in* substances, which can continue to exist whether they have it or not. Primary goodness is not *in* substances, but constitutes them *as* substances. Consider a person who is a glutton. Where we are using the term "person" as a count noun (like the term "armadillo") to explain persistence through change, we should not say that this person is any less a person or less a human being because she eats so much. She may be a larger human being, but large and small are equally human.

---

18. *Quodlibet* q.18, AW 169.

19. Primary goodness is "convertible with being," *Rep.* 2.34. q.un.n.18. Primary goods are essential, and secondary goods are accidental in the sense that the substance can be there without them. Primary goodness does have a hierarchy, since some kinds of substance are more perfect than others. But it does not come in different degrees to different members of the same species. An angel has more of this kind of being and goodness than an armadillo, but all armadillos have the same amount.

She has the primary goodness of being human in full, but she is lacking the secondary goodness of moderation.[20]

In the moral goodness passage Scotus goes on to divide secondary goodness itself into two. Secondary goodness always involves a relation. But we can say that one thing is good in the secondary sense because it is *appropriate* to another thing, or we can say that one thing is good in the secondary sense because it *has* a second thing. Scotus uses examples from Augustine, both of them examples of natural goods.[21] Health is good in a secondary sense because it is *appropriate* to an animal. A man's face is good in a secondary sense if he *has* regular features, a cheerful expression, and a glowing color. The moral goodness of an act is a secondary goodness of this second kind. The act is morally good because it *has* "all that the agent's right reason declares must pertain to the act or the agent in acting." This is a phrase that needs unpacking. Scotus is saying that for an act to be morally good, it has to be prescribed or willed by the agent.[22] This means that only free or willed acts can be morally good, and only if they are carried out for the sake of the willed end or purpose. If we take the act of a person eating, for example, it can have an appropriate object, namely "food capable of restoring what man has lost." A stone would not be an appropriate object, and nor would hay (though this might be appropriate for a cow eating).[23] The eating be-

20. We can perhaps say that a person who has become a slave to food has become "less a person," but the term "person" inside this latter phrase is no longer being used as a count noun.

21. Scotus uses the term "natural" for both primary and secondary goods.

22. Scotus, *Quodlibet* q.18, AW 170.

23. Having an appropriate object in this way brings an act into the right genus for moral goodness, Scotus says, but the act does not yet have moral specification. This is consistent with the view of Aquinas at ST Ia-IIae 18, article 4. See Thomas Gilbey's note in the Blackfriars edition, vol. 18, pp. 16-17. There is an apparent difference in doctrine, because Aquinas says that the genus is the action's being an action; but it is what I have called "primary goodness" that is in question here, and an act is not good *simpliciter* without the goodness of the intended end.

longs to the right kind for being morally good, however, only if the object is willed in the right way. Suppose an armadillo eats an ant. We might say that it is doing so in pursuit of a natural good. But the object in this case is not chosen freely, since the armadillo does not have the affection for justice; and in the absence of the affection for justice, the affection for the natural good, the affection for the ant, is not free. A human being eating nutritious food, on the other hand, rather than a Twinkie, is characteristically choosing to do so with the right end or purpose. So we have here the right kind for what is morally good. Appropriateness is also required of the manner in which the action is performed, the time at which it is performed, and the place in which it is performed.[24] But the main moral specification comes from the agent's end. In particular, whether the act is morally good or morally bad depends on whether or not it comes from an end given by the agent's affection for justice, namely the love of an intrinsic good for its own sake.

5. Supervenience

A term in the moral goodness passage which I did not discuss is "supervenient." Actually the term comes in the Latin, *superveniens,* and not in the English translation I quoted. I am going to compare the meaning Scotus gives to this term with the meaning R. M. Hare, the prescriptivist, gives to it, in his account of the relation between evaluative and descriptive properties. R. M. Hare in fact introduced the term into twentieth-century analytic philosophy. I do not want to hang anything on the use of the term. It is not a technical term for Scotus. But the prescriptivist's account of the relation between eval-

24. See Aristotle, *Nicomachean Ethics* II, 9, 1109a25f.: "It is hard work to be excellent. . . . Getting angry, or giving and spending money, is easy and anyone can do it; but doing it to the right person, in the right amount, at the right time, for the right end, and in the right way is no longer easy, nor can anyone do it. Hence [doing these things] well is rare, praiseworthy and fine."

uation and description shares a common structure with Scotus's account of the relation between morality and nature. This common structure is, I hope, illuminating.[25] For we need a way to understand how Scotus can say two things together: first that morality cannot be deduced from nature and second that morality is grounded in nature. I think it is the genius of his view to say both of these things, but it is initially hard to see how they can be consistent. The supervenience relation gives us a helpful model. When I asked R. M. Hare if he took the term from Scotus, he denied it. He said he took it "from the air." But when I explained to him what I thought Scotus's view was, he said it was close to his own, and in fact he referred to Scotus as a predecessor in his final book.[26]

The term "supervenience" is used in other contexts in contemporary philosophy, such as the philosophy of mind, where its application seems to me mysterious. I will not be referring to those contexts. Here is R. M. Hare's account of how moral judgments, like other value judgments, acquire descriptive criteria: "[All such judgments] are made for reasons: that is, because of *something about* the subject of the judgment. Acts cannot be good or wrong just because they are good or wrong; there must be properties other than their goodness or wrongness which make them so. This feature of value judgments is sometimes called 'supervenience.' . . . That moral properties supervene on non-moral properties means simply that acts etc., have the moral properties because they have the non-moral properties ('It is wrong because it was an act of inflicting pain for fun'), although the moral property is not the same property as the non-moral property, nor even entailed by it. Someone

25. I am not claiming that supervenience relates the same terms in the two philosophers, but that there is the same structure. R. M. Hare is talking about the supervenience of evaluation on factual description. Scotus is talking about the supervenience of moral goodness on natural goodness (of one value on another).

26. R. M. Hare, *Objective Prescriptions and Other Essays* (Oxford: Clarendon Press, 1999), p. 77.

who said that it was an act of inflicting pain for fun but not wrong would not be contradicting himself, though most of us would call him immoral." This feature "does not forbid the adoption of different moral standards by different people; it simply prohibits a single person from adopting inconsistent standards at the same time, and says that (the standards) *will* be inconsistent if he says conflicting things about situations which he agrees to be identical in their universal properties."[27]

Supervenience in prescriptivism has a twofold negative side and a positive side. The negative side is the denial of the entailment from description to evaluation and the denial of the entailment from evaluation to description. Inflicting pain for fun is wrong. But describing the act as inflicting pain for fun does not entail evaluating it as wrong or *vice versa*. In the first chapter I talked about the strawberry's being good and sweet. You are not logically required to judge that it is good just because you have judged that it is sweet or *vice versa*. Why is this? It is because judging a strawberry to be good or an act to be wrong is, on this account, prescriptive. Such judgments standardly express some act or disposition that belongs within the family of emotion, desire, and will. This was the central truth of expressivism as I described it in the first chapter.[28] The agent describes an act, let us say, as inflicting pain for fun. It simply does not follow that she is against it or for it. This is still logically an open question, though *she* may have settled it before giving the description, and *we* may have settled that being against gratuitous torture is necessary for a morally good person. We can see this point by noting that a fallen angel, or for that matter the Marquis de Sade, might give the description of an act as inflicting pain for fun as a *recommendation* of the act. Another way to see this is to return to the thought experiment that Scotus borrows from Anselm. An angel who had the

---

27. R. M. Hare, *Sorting Out Ethics* (Oxford: Clarendon Press, 1997), p. 21.

28. This is different from saying that the judgment reports the fact that the maker of the judgment has performed such an act of the will. In the first chapter I described both G. E. Moore and A. J. Ayer making this point.

affection for advantage but not the affection for justice might know that an act was inflicting pain for fun. But this angel would not be free. So the judgment that the act was morally wrong would be impossible for such an angel on the prescriptivist picture of moral judgment, since this angel would not have made the free decision of the will that moral evaluation expresses. So it does not follow from the fact that the angel has knowledge of the descriptive property that the angel makes the relevant evaluation.

The positive side of supervenience is that the act nonetheless has the value property *because* it has the descriptive property. The act is wrong because it is inflicting pain for fun. The strawberry is good because it is sweet. One good way to illustrate the positive side of supervenience in the contemporary discussion is to make the analogy with causal properties. If one event causes another, there could not be a qualitatively identical situation in which the corresponding events were conjoined and *not* causally linked. This is the basis of the so-called "covering law" theory of causal explanation.[29] Causation is not, so to speak, arbitrary; and this follows from the supervenience of the causal property on the non-causal properties of the initial event. In the same way, it is the universal descriptive properties (the sweetness, firmness, and juiciness of the strawberry) that ground the evaluation ("The strawberry is good"). Once an agent is committed to an evaluation based on those descriptive properties, she is committed to the same judgment given the same descriptive universal properties. This kind of consistency is one hallmark of rationality; and it is built into the supervenience relation.

Prescriptivism thus says both that evaluation is not deducible from factual (non-evaluative) description or *vice versa*, and that evaluation is grounded on factual description. I am now going to try to show how Scotus displays this same structure, negative and positive, in the relations he establishes between morality and nature.

29. Carl Hempel, *Aspects of Scientific Explanation* (New York: Free Press, 1965), pp. 345f.

6. The Negative Side of Supervenience in Scotus

In Scotus the moral goodness or badness of an act supervenes on the act itself (together with its primary and secondary natural goodness). The armadillo that eats an ant is indeed fulfilling its nature and pursuing an object that is naturally good. But this is not yet the right species of act to be morally good. The morally good requires, in addition, that the natural good be willed. We can see in such an example the first denial required by supervenience. The armadillo is in some sense "judging" the ant to be good, but it does not follow that it is morally evaluating. The same would be true of an angel who judged something naturally good, but did not have the affection for justice. An act's being morally right is not entailed by the act's being directed towards a naturally good object.

Scotus would also deny that the judgment that an act is wrong (or right) entails that the act is directed towards any particular natural evil (or natural good). This denial requires, in Scotus, one qualification; but to see this, we need some more background in his overall theory.[30] The affection for justice is, he holds, an inclination toward intrinsic goods for their own sake, which means that it is an inclination towards God. For God is our end, and the final end of everything.[31] Even God is required (by God's justice) to love God. God is not required to create us. But if God does create us, the requirement of justice is that we be created such that union with God is our final end. In Scotus the final end for human beings is that we become co-

30. The qualification is that given Scotus's divine command theory, it will follow from an act's being right that it is willed by God. In the same way, given R. M. Hare's normative theory, it follows from an act's being right that it is prescribed by the archangel, and this is an exception to the supervenience claim that no fact is entailed.

31. "Anything other than God is good because God wills it and not vice versa," *Opus Oxon.* III.19. God is our end, "from whose goodness stems the moral goodness of any act that is a means to that end," *Ord.* III, suppl., dist. 27, art. 3, AW 284. See Effrem Bettoni, *Duns Scotus,* trans. Bernardine Bonansea (Washington, D.C.: Catholic University of America Press, 1961), p. 173.

lovers with God *(condiligentes),* entering into the love that is between the three persons of the Trinity. The rule of justice in us is thus something we "receive from a higher will," namely God's. In terms of the discussion in the first chapter, a divine command theorist can say that the pull *to* the good is a pull *by* God's call. We could use another piece of language from Iris Murdoch. God is the magnetic center. Just as the magnet attracts through the iron rings attached to it, so there are goods other than God to which we feel the pull. But it is the center of this attraction that holds all these goods together and coordinates them. Either the call will be directly to human union with God, or to something else which is God's selected route to this end. Here we have the distinction which Scotus sees between the first and second tables of the ten commandments.[32] The first table tells us our duties towards God, and the second our duties towards our neighbor. Scotus is inclined to say that the first table gives us the law of nature in the strict sense, but the second table does not.[33] "What pertains to the law of nature is either a practical principle known immediately from its terms or necessary conclusions that follow from such principles. In either case they possess necessary truth."[34] God is bound to love the divine essence, and (given that God creates others) to will that those others love it also. So the commandments that tell us to love God have the kind of necessity required for natural law in the strict sense, but the commandments that tell us how to love our neighbor do not. They are extremely fitting, Scotus says, but still contingent.[35]

32. In Scotus's list, the first table is composed of the first three commandments and the second of the last seven. He is counting the commandment about the Sabbath as the third, and dividing the commandment about coveting into the command not to covet the neighbor's wife (commandment nine) and the commandment not to covet the rest of what belongs to the neighbor (commandment ten).

33. Scotus hesitates about the third commandment, especially the *seventh day. Ord.* III, suppl., dist. 37, AW 203.

34. *Ord.* III, suppl., dist. 37, AW 199.

35. Scotus is not saying that love of the neighbor is contingently com-

This is because God is not, for Scotus, limited in the ways in which we can be ordered to our final end. We do not know that God is constrained to will that we reach this end, for example, by following the second table of the law. The following suggestions are mine and not Scotus's. Consider the natural good of reproduction and the command to honor one's parents. Perhaps God could have willed that humans did not reproduce, but (let us say) appeared spontaneously in the condition of a present day seventeen-year-old. The point of this example is that our human nature could be, in this very different world, the same as it is here, with no change to our capacity to reproduce sexually. Perhaps celibacy is a way to express one's sexuality, and not merely the absence of a specific kind of sexual activity.[36] If so, it could be normative in such a world for everyone. The reply might be that God in our world gives a special gift of celibacy, and thereby shows that it is not normative for everyone. But God does not change our nature in giving us such a gift. What I am objecting to is the *deduction* of the ten commandments from our created nature. In some versions of natural law theory, if we know the truths about our nature, the injunctions *follow*. Perhaps God could have willed also that we did not talk to each other, but transcended even conceptualization in a kind of shared wordless contemplation of God like the kind Pseudo-Dionysius attributes to the higher orders of angels. Perhaps God could have willed that we did not own property, but shared all things in common, assigning use as each had need.[37] Perhaps (to get more bizarre) God could have willed that we

---

manded (given the creation of the neighbor), but that the form in which this love is to be shown is contingent. See *Ord.* III, suppl., dist. 28, AW 288-89.

36. This is often not understood. See Kathleen Norris, *The Cloister Walk* (New York: Riverhead Books, 1996), and Gladys Verhulst, "A Celibate and Intimate Life," *Perspectives* 14, no. 5 (May 1999): 4-7.

37. Scotus says, "Given the principle of positive law that life in a community or state ought to be peaceful, it does not follow from this necessarily that everyone ought to have possessions distinct from those of another, for peace could reign in a group or among those living together, even if everything was

kill each other at the age of eighteen, at which point God would immediately bring us back to life. (This would put us into the situation of Abraham and Isaac, at least on one traditional version of this story, in which Abraham believed that both he and Isaac would be returning down the mountain, and told his servants so.)[38] All of this may seem like idle speculation. (Karl Barth warns us against the possible idolatry in the thought of what God could have done.) I am not claiming that we know that God could have willed all these things, but that we do not know that God could not have. The point is that there is no necessary connection between our created natures and the way we reach our final end. None of the commandments in the second table of the law would apply to us in this very different world I have imagined, but, if I am right, there is no impossibility in the supposition that our nature remains the same. As things are, however, God has willed that we reach our final end in the way that the ten commandments specify. God has willed, moreover, that we live this way in order to reach our final end. This is, so to speak, the route God has ordained.

I want to explore this metaphor of a route for a moment, for I think it is illuminating, and I will use it several times in the rest of this chapter. Imagine a parent who constructs a treasure hunt for her son. The whole house and garden is transformed into a setting for the game, with clues hidden in various places, some leading to each other sequentially, and others giving collateral information independently of each other. If the child finds that he cannot solve some of the clues, he can always go to his mother for advice, but the goal is that he do it himself. Some things he knows not from written clues, but just from knowing the layout of the house and

---

common property. Not even in the case of the infirm is private possession an absolute necessity." *Ord.* III, suppl. dist. 37, AW 200. These examples are harder to construct if we add in the positive versions of the ten commandments that can be found, for example, in the Heidelberg Catechism (and also in Calvin). But even here, I would defend the denial of necessity.

38. See Hebrews 11:19 and Genesis 22:5.

garden. The final clue leads to where the final treasure is hidden (though there may be other smaller treasures along the way). In some lucky families, it happens that the final treasure is not really the point of the game, though it is the *internal* point of it. The game itself has a higher end, external to it, which is that the child and his parent enjoy each other. The mother enjoys each stage of the child's discovery, and he enjoys her enjoyment, and after the game is over it is this mutual delight that has been the greatest good. It is true that this end will be frustrated if the child does not find the treasure, but that is just part of the mechanics of the game, not what gives the game its point. In other less lucky families the treasure is after all the main point, and a disappointingly small treasure can ruin the whole thing.

God's arrangements for our good might be like this. There is no necessary way the parent has to set up the game, though the final end consisting in some form of union is necessary. Once the clues are set up, then the route to the treasure is indeed set (though we could change the analogy, if we wanted to accommodate the possibility of some changes in the routing), and it is our task to discover it. Our natural happiness might be like the treasure, the internal end of the hunt. Perhaps there is a kind of life that is reached by truth-telling and parent-honoring and so on, and we discover that when we live this way we make progress, and the world makes moral sense to us. If we will to live this way, we are recapitulating in our wills God's will for our willing. But we should not deceive ourselves that we have discovered something that is necessitating God's will for our willing; that God had to will this way given the creation of beings with human nature. Finally, it is possible, as in the treasure hunt, to be inordinately attached to the treasure that is the internal end of the game. As Scotus says of Lucifer, it is possible to "want the beatific object (happiness) to belong exclusively to himself, rather than to be in another, such as in his God."[39]

39. *Ord.* II, dist. 6, q.2, AW 300.

One complication here is that Scotus also holds that being co-lovers with God is the proper perfection or happiness of a human being, and so humans are naturally moved towards it. This means that the analogy of the treasure hunt is misleading. For it implies a separation between the treasure (our natural happiness) and the point of the game (the mutual enjoyment of parent and child). In Scotus's view, these two are in fact united, but our love of God can be motivated in importantly different ways. He discusses three manners in which we might be drawn towards our final end.[40] We might love God intrinsically even if God did not unite with us. We might love God, secondly, because God unites with us. And we might love God, thirdly, because of what Scotus calls the "satisfaction" of happiness. The first kind of love is charity, whose primacy among the theological virtues Scotus wants to defend. He says that this kind of love does not desire the good of the lover insofar as it benefits the lover, but is an activity that tends to the object for its own sake, and would do so even if, to assume the impossible, all benefit for the lover were excluded. This is the counterfactual I mentioned above in connection with Luther and generations of Presbyterian ministers. Scotus illustrates the difference between the first and the second kind of love by a distinction within human friendship. Someone is properly first loved because of herself, and only secondarily because she returns our love. So too with God. The difference between the second and the third kind of love is that the "satisfaction" that God gives us is a consequence or accompaniment of the act of loving God. It is an inevitable accompaniment, but it is not itself our proper aim. So the affection for advantage is drawn towards union with God, but only in the second and third ways, not (as the affection for justice) in the first and best way.

It might be objected that the moral life is not a game, in the way that I presented the picture of the treasure hunt as a game. In the treasure hunt it is entirely up to the parent where to put the treasure,

---

40. *Ord.* III, suppl. dist. 27, art. 1, AW 277.

what to write in the clues, and where to hide them. The objection is that God's choice of route for us is not discretionary in this way, because God is using the route to reveal the divine nature to people like us. Thus Calvin says, "God has so depicted his character in the law that if any man carries out in deeds whatever is enjoined there, he will express the image of God, as it were, in his own life."[41] Thus the commandment to be faithful in marriage represents to us God's character of faithfulness to those within the covenant. The commandment not to bear false witness represents to us God's character of revealing truth in Scripture and in the life of Christ. The route for us is thus no more accidental than these features of God's character. In reply to this objection, we should make a distinction between the necessity of what is revealed and the necessity of the revealing of it. Even if it is granted that God does reveal the divine nature through commands to people like us, and that God necessarily has the character which is so revealed, it does not follow that God reveals this character necessarily. Consider again the picture of the treasure hunt. It may be that the mother reveals her character through her clues. Perhaps some of them are witty, and show her sense of humor, and others of them are learned (with abstruse quotations), and others poetic. But it does not follow that she necessarily reveals her wit or her learning or her sensibility. She could have revealed quite other parts of her character, or chosen not to reveal her character through her clues at all. Even if we concede, then, that God's commands are fitted to reveal God's character to people like us, it does not follow that these commands are necessary given our nature. Natural law theory, if it claims the connection *is* necessary, is wrong.

By conducting the kind of thought experiment I suggested earlier about celibacy and the end of private property and killing eighteen-year-olds, we can see that the commandments of the second table are neither necessary practical principles of the right kind to be natural law strictly speaking, nor do they follow from such princi-

41. *Institutes* 2.8.51.

ples. Scotus reinforces this conclusion by producing examples where God "dispenses" from these commandments. To dispense, here, is either to revoke or clarify. In the case of the ceremonial laws (for example about kosher food), God *revoked* them, according to Scotus. In cases like Abraham and the commandment on killing, it seems that God is also revoking, though this is complicated by the possibility that Abraham believed that Isaac would come back to life.[42] If God revoked the prohibition against killing in the case of Abraham, it follows that this commandment is not necessary, because then it would be binding on God even in that particular case. The commandments are, rather, within God's discretion (in Latin, his *arbitrium*). It is almost inevitable that we put this in English by saying that God's decision is "arbitrary," but this is misleading in the current ordinary sense of the word. The negative connotation of the term arises from its implication that there is a reason for a given decision which is not being given due weight.[43] It is only in the technical and unfamiliar legal sense that these principles are arbitrary, and even then God's willing is not (for Scotus) without reason, for the principles are chosen by God as a route to our final end.[44] This is the Scotist reply to

42. Dispensing by clarifying means showing some universal property which makes an otherwise forbidden act permissible. In the case of Abraham and Isaac, on the traditional interpretation I have already mentioned, Abraham believed that both he and his son would be returning down the mountain. The actual act of killing an innocent person (his son moreover) was still the same in kind as the act of child-killing which the Bible condemns in the surrounding cultures, but Abraham's belief was that God would somehow miraculously change the results of this act. But the distinction here between the act itself and its results is imprecise.

43. The *Oxford English Dictionary* has "derived from mere opinion; capricious; unrestrained; despotic. (Law) discretionary." Calvin denies that God is arbitrary at *Institutes* 3.23.2.

44. See Robert Prentice, "The Contingent Element Governing the Natural Law on the Last Seven Precepts of the Decalogue, According to Duns Scotus," *Antonianum* 42 (1967): 285. "God wills them as an efficacious means of leading man to his final end." But if we ask *why* God chose the particular route he did, this is for Scotus a sign of our own lack of maturity (*indisciplinati,*

one of the standard objections to divine command theory, that it makes morality arbitrary.

We cannot deduce the goodness of the act from our nature *even if we add* a description of the situation.[45] Scotus makes this point by distinguishing between moral goodness and conforming to God's will.[46] On the view I have been pressing, you might think that Scotus would say that doing the morally right thing is repeating or recapitulating God's will in our willing. But the subtle doctor is more careful. He gives the example of those who willed that Christ should suffer and die, something that Christ himself also willed (since his Father did not let that cup pass from him). Nonetheless those who willed this sinned, as Christ showed by asking his Father to forgive them. What we are to repeat is not just God's willing, but God's willing for our willing. And it is *this* which God reveals when giving us the second table of the law, our route to our final good. We can, therefore, in this limited way know what it is right to do. But we have to preserve a proper sense of humility about this knowledge. It is not

---

Ord. I.8.5/23-24). Does it follow from this that we know nothing about what route God could have prescribed? Must we say that he could have commanded bestiality as the expression of our sexuality? I think the best attitude here is to say that we simply do not know what he could have commanded and what he could not.

45. This can be understood again with relation to the negative feature of supervenience. I said that from the knowledge that an act a moral property (e.g., moral goodness), we do not know that the act is directed to any particular natural good or set of goods other than God. We can now ask what happens if we add the description of the situation in which the act is performed. Suppose that I know that an agent has done a morally good act in a situation where a child is drowning, and in which nothing miraculous is going to occur, such as the child coming back to life. How could I know such a thing? This is unclear, but suppose I do know it. I will then know that the act, because it is morally good, is aimed (both in object and in end) at the final good of the affected parties. Does it follow that I know that the agent has saved the child's life? No, it does not. For it is always possible that the child's final good is in this situation to go straight to union with God.

46. *Ord.* I, dist. 48, AW 181-82.

knowledge of a necessity binding God's will for our situation, but of a contingent ordination. It is no doubt more comfortable to believe that the morally right thing to do is strictly required (even for God's willing) by the combination of our nature and the situation. But we are not entitled to this belief. Moreover there is a certain gratitude occasioned by the thought that God gave us this route even though God did not have to do so.

Here, then, is the second denial within the negative structure of supervenience. A moral judgment links a naturally good object with an end internal to the affection for justice (namely, to our final end as something good in itself). But having union with God as our end does not by itself require that any particular natural good protected in the second table of the law is the way to reach this end. It is still up to God to determine which goods to ordain as the route by which we become co-lovers. So from the knowledge that an act has a moral property (e.g., moral goodness), we do not know that the act is directed to any particular natural good or set of goods other than God.

7. The Positive Side

There is also the positive side of supervenience. If the negative side emphasizes the freedom involved in moral evaluation, the positive side emphasizes the rationality involved in it. Maybe the moral law towards the neighbor does not *follow* from our nature, but it *fits* it spectacularly well. We can see this best when we flourish after keeping the law and when we deteriorate after breaking it.

In the terms that Scotus uses, he wants to insist that "God wills in a most reasonable and orderly manner."[47] Since the usual objection to divine command theories in ethics is that they make moral judgment arbitrary in the pejorative sense, this is an important

---

47. *Deus est rationabilissime et ordinatissime volens. Opus Oxon.* III, dist. 32, q.un.n. 6.

point. I want to argue that Scotus is committed to a view that "grounds ethics in nature," and I have now presented the background material that will enable me to do this.[48] The first point is that God necessarily, according to Scotus, loves the goodness of the divine nature. "Indeed, the divine essence, which is the primary object of (God's) will, is to be willed in itself. Hence that will necessarily and correctly wills that object which is properly to be willed in itself."[49] Secondly, God wills to have co-lovers, and the principle "God is to be loved" applies necessarily also to those creatures.[50] God is not necessitated to create; but "whatever God made, you know that God has made it with right reason," which means that God has necessarily ordered it towards the divine nature, the primary good.[51] From this come the commandments in the first table of the Decalogue (with a hesitation about the seventh day in what Scotus lists as the third commandment).

When we come to the second table of the Decalogue, however, there is no longer the sort of necessity that enables us to call this

48. Mary Elizabeth Ingham argues that in Scotus the good operates through intention as an integral efficient cause (not final) and as such the end "has no objective existence exterior to the will," in *Ethics and Freedom: An Historical-Critical Investigation of Scotist Ethical Thought* (Lanham, Md.: The University Press of America, 1989), p. 161. She goes on to say that Scotus "presents the rational finite will as constitutive of moral goodness in a way similar to (the way he presents) the divine will as creative of goodness." This reading makes Scotus a creative anti-realist, like Christine Korsgaard and J. B. Schneewind, whose views I discuss in chapter three. On my view, it is true both that normative ethics is founded on nature and that there is no deduction of the first from the second. The content of the second table as well as its force is due to the divine will, and neither of these is entailed by human nature. My view is also different from that of Coplestone, who argues that for Scotus "it is not the content of the moral law which is due to the divine will, but the obligation of the moral law, its morally binding force," in *A History of Philosophy III* (Garden City, N.Y.: Doubleday/Image Books, 1985), p. 547.

49. *Opus Oxon.* I, dist. 10, q.un.n. 11.

50. *Ord.* III, suppl., dist. 28, AW 288. See also AW 20.

51. *Rep.* 1 A, dist. 44, q.2, AW 19.

God's Commands

strictly natural law (known immediately from its terms, or deduced from principles which are known that way). There are innumerable ways God could have ordered us towards union, even given the nature with which we were created. The route God has in fact chosen is binding upon us because God has chosen it. But we can still say that the route is good *because* it takes us to our final end, and is thus fitted to our nature. This is the positive side of the supervenience relation.

God's commands or call fit our nature, both our human nature and our individual nature. The command not to bear false witness fits the human being's deep-seated desire to share life together with other humans on the basis of verbal communication. It is a presupposition of such communication that the speaker is communicating what she believes to be the truth. We find out when we lie that we have damaged the life we share together. What is right is also what makes for flourishing as a human being. This much is common to Scotus and the deductivist natural law tradition. They differ in the logical relations they see between human nature and the moral law. Scotus believes also in individual natures. I have not emphasized this part of his theory, but it is distinctive. There is a "thisness," in Latin *haecceitas,* for each substance, which God knows and we do not. It is this feature of his thought which inspired Gerard Manley Hopkins's notion of "inscape," and it is expressed in some of Hopkins's greatest poems, such as "God's Grandeur," "Windhover," "Binsey Poplars," "Duns Scotus's Oxford," "Henry Purcell," and "Inversnaid." The "thisness" can be associated with the name of each one of us, written on a white stone, which we are told in the book of Revelation God knows but we do not yet know. The individual name gives the individual haecceity. God's call to us is to grow into this individual character.[52] Sometimes this call will be by way of congruence with what we already are and sometimes by way of dissonance. Sometimes just by being the person I am in the situation I am, I am enabled to do

---

52. I am going beyond Scotus in the ethical use I am making of the notion of haecceity.

God's work. But sometimes the call is to face a characteristic weakness, and we are put into a situation in which it is only by facing this that we can do what is good. The individual call to two people in the same situation can be to face opposite weaknesses. Thus in one and the same story Jairus, the ruler of the synagogue, had to wait for the woman with a hemorrhage and surrender control while his daughter was dying, and the woman had to make herself and her shame public to the whole crowd.[53] The story can be interpreted this way: Neither of them had the inclination yet (Jairus for patience or the woman for publicity), and the character God was calling them to had to be formed in them through opposition to the inclinations they did have.

8. The Eudaimonist Objection

I will end by replying to an important set of objections made by the eudaimonist to the view I have been describing. Eudaimonism is the view that makes all motivation derivative from an agent's own happiness. Here is one statement of the view: "And so the will naturally tends towards its own last end, for every man naturally wills beatitude. And from this natural willing are caused all other willings, since whatever a man wills, he wills on account of the end."[54] Scotus gives us a

53. Luke 8:40-56.
54. Thomas Aquinas, ST I, q.20. a.2. It is, however, a vexed question how to interpret Thomas here. See, for example, A. Wohlman, "Amour du bien propre et amour de soi dans la doctrine thomiste de l'amour," *Revue Thomiste* 81 (1981): 204-34; Scott MacDonald, "Egoistic Rationalism: Aquinas's Basis for Christian Morality," in *Christian Theism and the Problems of Philosophy*, ed. Michael Beaty (1989); and David Gallagher, "Thomas Aquinas on Self-Love as the Basis for Love of Others," *Acta Philosophica* (Rome, 1999). This last paper puts the point in a way that clarifies the contrast with Scotus: "I love God . . . not just because God is the best thing there is. I love God because he is the source of my goodness and because I find in God my own goodness in the highest degree." But with the affection of justice, Scotus would say, I do love

way to attack eudaimonism, by making the affection for justice central to obligation rather than the affection for advantage. But the eudaimonist is not yet defeated. There is indeed a eudaimonist strain within the Augustinian tradition to which Scotus belongs.[55] I am not claiming to have solved the difficulties here, but I can carry the argument a few steps further. There is something in eudaimonism which is unacceptably self-regarding. Scotus is not here urging the disappearance of the affection for advantage. He is not a quietist, of the type defined in the condemnation by Pope Innocent XII, those who support "the proposition that there is a habitual state of love of God which is pure charity without any admixture of the motive of self-interest, in which the fear of punishments, and the desire for reward, has no part, and in which God is not loved for any happiness to be found in loving him."[56] Rather, the good in heaven "neither were able, nor wished, to dislike having happiness, or to have no desire for it. But they did not want it more than they wanted God to have everything good." It is a question, in other words, not of the disappearance of the affection for advantage, but of its ranking below the affection for justice. What is wrong with eudaimonism is that it makes happiness central. Scotus is urging that the self leave the throne and offer it to God.[57]

God just because God is the best thing there is. I will not try to attribute views to Thomas in what follows, but I will try to state what seem to me the strongest objections to Scotus.

55. See, for example, Augustine's *De Libero Arbitrio* IX.26: "In so far as all men seek the happy life they do not err. . . . Everyone is happy who attains the chief good, which indisputably is the end which we all desire."

56. Discussed in Anthony Kenny, *Aristotle on the Perfect Life* (Oxford: Clarendon Press, 1992), p. 54.

57. Scotus has two different notions of freedom, and it is hard to be clear about the relations between them. There is first a libertarian freedom, in which the will is a self-determining power for opposites. There is nothing that constrains the will, even the intellect, though the intellect has weight *(pondus)* with the will. The will is indeterminate, like matter, except that matter is indeterminate by insufficiency and the will by superabundance. On the other hand there is a moral freedom, which is a kind of steadfastness *(firmitas)* and is above the

I will raise and then reply to three eudaimonist objections to the Scotist position. First, the Bible is full of expressions of a reciprocal relationship between God and the people of the covenant. We love God and God blesses us, and we trust God to bless us. The idea that we should somehow separate our love for God from this expectation is not itself based in Scripture.[58] It is based on an abstract and impersonal view of God. Scotus thinks of God as infinite being, and he thinks of the affection for justice as giving such a being its due, so that the good of a finite being is incommensurable with this infinity. But the biblical picture is rather of God as father, or king, or friend, and relationships of this kind are based on (different degrees of) mutuality. It is the Aristotelian not the biblical God whose perfection "consists in being superior to thinking of anything beside himself."[59] Even an extreme statement like Job's, "Though he slay me, yet will I trust in him," while it looks like the kind of counterfactual that Scotus relies upon, is in fact a paradoxical expression of trust even in the face of death, and trust is unintelligible without the expectation of good from the person trusted.[60] So far the objection.

In reply, we should say that Christ tells us that the first commandment is to love God with *all* our heart and mind and soul and strength. It is true that he goes on to say that we should love the neighbor as the self, so that the total dedication to God does not preclude all other attachments. But it is important that Christ does not say we should love God as the self. Indeed Christ (unlike Lucifer, in the account Scotus gives) did not count equality with God a thing to be grasped, but emptied himself, and Paul recommends this empty-

---

possibility of wrongful choice. I take it that Scotus is committed to libertarian freedom, and one of his objections to eudaimonism is that it deprives us of this. See Thomas Williams, "The Libertarian Foundations of Scotus's Moral Philosophy," *The Thomist* 62, no. 2 (April 1998): 193-215, especially 199ff.

58. For example, we are told to be like Jesus who endured the cross "for the joy set before him" (Hebrews 12:2).

59. *Eudemian Ethics* VII, 12, 1245b17.

60. Job 13:15, but this may not be what the text means.

ing of the self as a model for us.[61] As Scotus says, we do in fact regard the sacrifice of self as a higher form of love. Kierkegaard describes the case of someone who prefers the good of the beloved even when it means destroying the relationship between them (and he may have been thinking of his own relationship with Regina). Perhaps it is only because of sin that we have to make this kind of choice. But nevertheless, faced with such choice, we do think the self-emptying kind of love is higher. A good case is Paul's thought, in Romans 9:3, "For I could wish that I myself were cursed and cut off from Christ for the sake of my brothers, those of my own race." Paul is performing just the kind of counterfactual thought experiment that is required here. If his eternal destruction were necessary, which it isn't, for the well-being of his people, he would prefer his destruction.

A second objection is that Scotus is confusing the hope for happiness with selfishness. It is true that happiness contains a reference to the self (since it is one's own well-being). But concern for the self is not necessarily selfish. One can see this in the Aristotelian picture, in which the agent's own flourishing requires the flourishing of the agent's family, friends, and city. It is as though the self is elastic, coming to include more and more other people within the scope of its self-related concern. It becomes a "we-self" as opposed to a "me-self." Aristotle starts this development within the family. "A parent loves his children as (he loves) himself. For what has come from him is a sort of other himself; (it is other because) it is separate."[62] This "other self" relation within the family is then extended to virtuous friends, who also become other selves.[63] There is no reason in principle why the relationship with God should not be construed in these terms, and this is exactly what the pictures of God as father, king, and friend suggest. So far the objection.

In reply to the second objection, we should say that the "we-self"

61. Philippians 2:5.
62. *Nicomachean Ethics* VIII, 12, 1161b28f., Irwin's translation.
63. *Ibid.*, IX, 4, 1166a30f.

is still unacceptably self-regarding. It does not recognize the claims of the "other." In Aristotle, this is manifested by his failure to extend the moral sphere to all human beings as such.[64] But even if we make the self sufficiently elastic to embrace all human beings, still the claim of the other *as* other is denied. God should be loved not merely to the extent that we have appropriated God, but also to the extent that we have not. Scotus uses counterfactuals to make this vivid to us. Suppose God did not enter into union with us. Would we love God anyway? The extension of the "me-self" to the "we-self" is based by Aristotle on similarity. The father recognizes himself in his child, and the friend finds in his friend the same commitment to the good. But morality requires the respect for difference. In terms of our relationship to God, there are times when we understand what we see of divine action and we feel kinship, and there are other times when God seems quite remote and alien. We are called to love God in those times where we do not see the affinity. And the same is true in our relations to other people. We are supposed to love our *enemies*. To make happiness central is to insist on the primacy of the relation of others to the self over what those others are in themselves, independently of the self, and this is unacceptably self-regarding.[65]

A third objection is that Scotus is confusing the nature of an agent's concern with the explicit content of an agent's purposes. It may well be that self-concern has to be, so to speak, self-effacing, in order to reach its goal.[66] It is a familiar point about pleasure, to take

64. Cicero, *De Finibus* 3.63. But see Aristotle, *Nichomachean Ethics,* VIII, 11, 1161b6-8.

65. I am indebted here to a discussion with Linda Zagzebski; and I have been influenced by Emmanuel Levinas, who objects to Heidegger that "the fear for the other does not have this return to the self" (*Ethics and Infinity* [Pittsburgh: Duquesne University Press, 1985], p. 119).

66. This is one way to take Aquinas, ST II-II, q.26, a.3, ad 3, that one adverts less and less to the self, being more and more consumed by the goodness of God. But the question is whether at the end of such a process we have a genuine case of self-love at all. It is only the eudaimonist picture that forces such a description.

a parallel case, that if we pursue it as the focus of our efforts, we will not get it. In the long run it comes only as a side-effect of other things pursued for their own sake. But this does not mean that we have to pretend we do not that know this side-effect is in the offing. We have to allow ourselves to pursue these other things as the focus of our efforts and energies (say, playing a Mozart piano sonata as well as possible), knowing all the while that if we succeed, there is the prospect of moments of supreme pleasure. In the same way, the concern for the self may have to be self-effacing in order to reach its goal. With other people and with God we may have to pursue their good as the focus of our efforts, not concentrating on our own benefit even in the elastic sense just described. If I focus on my friend's good as a means to my own good or even as partially constituting my own good, I will probably not achieve the kind of surrender of myself to his good that makes for the very best relationship, and hence will defeat my own good. But this does not mean that I have to pretend *not* to know all along in the background that his good produces my good as well. The same is true in our relationship to God. So far the objection.

In reply to the third objection, we should say that either there is a kind of self-deception in the proposed self-effacement of self-interest, or we do not have a genuine case of self-love. If happiness is central, then our attachment to other things in themselves must be secondary. It is true that we can focus on the secondary, and leave the primary as background knowledge. We do this, for example, when we concentrate on the pictures on the ceiling in a dentist's office, which are put there just so that we can be distracted from what is happening inside our mouths. We know perfectly well that the pictures have this instrumental value, and that this is more important than their intrinsic interest, but we focus our energies and attention on them nonetheless. It is also true that the secondary goods do not have to be means to the primary, but can be constitutive of the primary. An excellent concert, for example, can be constituted of several less than wonderful pieces juxtaposed in an interesting way, and we would not say that the separate pieces are a means to the excellence of the whole. But if a good is secondary, although we can indeed pursue it for its own sake, we cannot without self-deception make it central. So if another person's welfare is constitutive of my happiness, but my happiness is central, the commitment I have to that person's welfare is always conditional on its constituting my happiness. This conditionality is built into the structure of eudaimonism, and it is this conditionality that is unacceptably self-regarding. If it is not built in, then we do not have a genuine case of self-love.

9. The Project So Far

To sum up, Scotus insists on the distinction between what God does and what God has to do. On the view this chapter has been defending, God's call to us does prescribe a reality independent of our prescribing it, namely the divinely chosen route to our final end. By saying that the reality is independent of our prescribing it, I mean that the route is there whether we try to follow it or not. It is objective, to use the term from the first chapter. But saying that the route has independent reality is not saying that it has necessity. There is a hypothetical necessity, in that once God has prescribed it, it is necessary for us to follow it if we are to reach the end. But there is no necessity for God's prescription of this route rather than some other, even given the creation of human nature. On the version of divine command theory I have given in this chapter, God's choosing this route is what makes it the right route.

In the example I gave in the introduction, Peter hears God's call in the pull of the relationship with Sue back towards reconciliation. The call is to a kind of faithfulness, which is like God's faithfulness to us. Peter has heard stories throughout his life about God's merciful dealings with our rejection and contempt. He has been taught that God requires faithfulness within human covenants, which imitate our covenant with God. Even though his nat-

84

ural inclinations are prompting him towards escape and with-drawal, he has a sense that this would be deeply wrong; and he acknowledges an authority here that comes from his recognition that the source of the call is God. He has the faith that obedience will in the end be best for him, but this is not why he is going to do it. Rather, he feels that this is what he *has* to do, and he would try to do it even if he thought it would finish him off. He has to do it because God has told him to.

In the third chapter I will talk about our response to this call, and that will take us back to the subjective pole of valuation. I will conduct the discussion in terms of helpful and unhelpful ways of thinking about human autonomy, and I will be focusing historically on the figure of Immanuel Kant.

Chapter Three

HUMAN AUTONOMY

1. Kant on Religion and Morality

In the second chapter I focused historically on someone I think is a friend of divine command theory, John Duns Scotus. In this final chapter I am going to focus on someone who is often construed as an enemy, namely Immanuel Kant. The lecture series that formed the basis for this book was named for Henry Stob. When I first arrived to teach at Calvin College, I used Henry Stob's book *Ethical Reflections* in my Ethics class, and I was able to talk to him about it. We talked mainly about moral realism, and various forms of it. One of the things we disagreed about was Kant. Henry Stob construes Kant, quite rightly in my view, as denying that theology precedes ethics. But then Stob continues: "(Kant) was not really removing the theological support of ethics; he was merely altering the underlying theology by unseating the Christian God and placing Rational Law upon the empty throne. God was made subject to Law; and in that instant Law itself became a god and began to determine the Kantian ethic."[1] There is truth in what Stob says here, but I am going to object to the "empty throne" idea. I think Kant continued to believe and urged us to believe that a personal God exists, and that we

---

1. Henry Stob, *Ethical Reflections* (Grand Rapids: Eerdmans, 1978), p. 37.

should recognize our duties as God's commands. Kant has been demonized as the presiding genius of modernism, or "the enlightenment project," which has in turn been seen as the Babylon where the remnants of the true church have been forced into exile. But it falsifies his views to make him into this kind of symbol.

We need to winnow. In the ancient world, and still in some places today, wheat is beaten or flailed, and then thrown up into the air, where the chaff is caught by the wind and blown away, and the grain, being heavier, descends into the fan. With Kant's work we can do the same: first disassemble it into its multitude of components, and then throw them up into the air so that the wind can carry away what is mere husk, and what is nutritious and good for us falls back to earth. This is much better than simply rejecting him. We can hold on to his very real merits; but we can also say to his contemporary secular followers, "Yes, there are these great merits. But when we enter into his system from the inside, rather than reading into him our own preferences, we can see that the system depends on a large number of traditional theistic assumptions. If we abandon these assumptions, the system simply doesn't work." In this way we can both be *better* interpreters of Kant, and lead the discussion back to the fundamental truths of the tradition that he tried and sometimes failed to incorporate. This is a strategy we need to use not only in the study of Kant's ethics, but of his philosophy generally. Even more broadly, we need to correct a prevailing pattern in the interpretation of the great classics of modern philosophy as a whole. There has been a tendency to see modern philosophy as aimed at the death of God and the death of metaphysics heralded by Nietzsche at the end of the nineteenth century. The modern classics have accordingly been trimmed to fit this model by their twentieth-century admirers. This is shifting somewhat in the last decade or so, and we are starting to see a new type of Kant scholarship that is much more faithful to his Christian background and continuing sympathies.[2] But if you read most of

2. Within Kant scholarship, this shift is signaled by *Kant's Philosophy of Re-*

the secondary literature of this century on Leibniz, or Descartes, just to take two examples, you will find a recurrent secularization that does violence to the intentions of the original authors. Thus, to take one notorious case, Bertrand Russell lays out the system of Leibniz without mentioning God in any one of the five original axioms. Why is this? It is because he admires Leibniz, and wants to do him a favor. All the Christian theology, which is everywhere apparent in Leibniz himself, is seen by Russell as an embarrassment, and is accordingly excluded.

I am going to focus on Kant's views about human autonomy. This is because he has given us an immensely influential argument, which is always taken as an argument from autonomy against the idea that we can think of God as the source of our moral obligation. It has been taken, together with a brief and impenetrable passage in Plato's *Euthyphro,* as a decisive rejection of the whole idea that what makes something obligatory for us is that God commands it.[3] I am going to show that those of Kant's successors who rely on it now as a refutation of divine command theory have misunderstood what

ligion Reconsidered, ed. Philip Rossi and Michael Wreen (Bloomington: Indiana University Press, 1991). Its editors start by questioning the commonly held views which "have generally held that this peripheral status [of Kant's treatment of religion] and lack of originality issued from the relentlessly reductionistic character of Kant's account, which sought to make religion — or at least those elements of religion which can be critically justified — wholly identical with or reducible to morality." A key work is J. B. Schneewind, *The Invention of Autonomy* (Cambridge: Cambridge University Press, 1998). Sources on other authors are Donald Rutherford, *Leibniz and the Rational Order of Nature* (Cambridge: Cambridge University Press, 1995), Robert M. Adams, *Leibniz: Determinist, Theist, Idealist* (Oxford: Oxford University Press, 1998), and James E. Force and Richard H. Popkin, eds., *The Books of Nature and Scripture: Recent Essays on Natural Philosophy, Theology and Biblical Criticism in the Netherlands of Spinoza's Time and the British Isles of Newton's Time* (Boston: Kluwer Academic, 1994).

3. For a statement of the problem with understanding the passage in the *Euthyphro* 10a1-11b5, see John E. Hare, *Plato's Euthyphro* (Bryn Mawr Commentaries, 1985), pp. 21-25.

Kant had in mind. I will end by showing that the usual contemporary interpretation of the argument is not only bad Kant exegesis but makes a bad argument as well.

I want to signal here some parts of the doctrine which I think are mistaken, some chaff for the wind to blow away. Kant suggests we think of revelation as two concentric circles. Historical revelation (for example, Scripture), which is given to particular people at particular times, belongs in the outer circle. Kant's project is to see if he can translate the items in this outer circle into the language of the inner circle, which is the revelation to reason, and is the same to all people at all times. So far I have no major objection.[4] But Kant holds out the prospect of identifying a content for the inner circle of revelation to reason that will eventually be sufficient without any outer circle of historical revelation at all. I doubt this, and it is not in any case consistent with another part of Kant's view which I am about to emphasize, that assistance is required from beyond human beings in order to accomplish a human life pleasing to God. I have explored this tension in Kant's thought in the second chapter of my book *The Moral Gap*. Also in *The Moral Gap* I have argued that Kant wrongly restricts the notion of what practical reason requires to the willing of universal law.[5] I think there are moral relations that are not expressible in terms of universal law. I also think Kant is wrong to assume that whenever there seems to be a conflict between the outer circle and the inner, between historical revelation and the revelation to reason, the inner circle wins. Here I think Henry Stob was right. Finally, I think Kant does not see what Duns Scotus saw about our final end. In Scotus obedience is a route to union with God. But in Kant there is no sense of this kind of union, and obedience or respect for the law remains as our end, together with happiness proportional to it.

So I am not following Kant uncritically. But I want to stress what I

4. *Religion* VI, 13. I will be making references to Kant by using the page numbers of the relevant volume of the Academy edition.

5. John E. Hare, *The Moral Gap* (Oxford: Clarendon Press, 1996), pp. 150-54.

call the vertical dimension of his moral thought. On my reading of Kant's project, he finds that there are some items in the outer circle which he cannot translate, but which he needs to continue to believe in order to have morality make rational sense. Conspicuous among these items is the belief in divine grace. Kant believes in a strong version of the doctrine of original sin, that we are born with a propensity to subordinate our duty to our own happiness. Kant also believes that we cannot by our own devices overcome this propensity, because it already underlies all our choices. We therefore require assistance from outside ourselves to accomplish what he calls "the revolution of the will," which reverses the priority, and which allows us to subordinate our happiness to our duty. Kant's candidate for this outside assistance is what he calls "a divine supplement," and he holds that we have to believe that this is available if we are to hold ourselves accountable to the moral law. Now this set of views is uncomfortable for many contemporary exegetes. Kant scholars try to rescue Kant from these embarrassing views by what I call "cushion hermeneutics." This is the strategy of suggesting that he did not really mean some of the things he says, but was saying them merely to cushion his disagreement with the authorities or perhaps his faithful old manservant.[6] But this kind of interpretation should be adopted only as a last resort, if there is no straightforward interpretation that fits the text. Especially this is true of Kant, who placed such a high value on sincerity.[7] This is what I meant earlier by saying that we can be better interpreters of Kant than his secularizing successors. We can adopt the principle that he means what he says, and that we should only interpret him some other way if we absolutely have to.

6. Allen Wood, "Kant's Deism," in *Kant's Philosophy of Religion Reconsidered*, pp. 1-21, 14. See also the phrase in E. Troeltsch, "utterances of prudence," quoted in Michel Despland, *Kant on History and Religion* (Montreal: McGill-Queen's University Press, 1973), p. 105, and the phrase "cover techniques" in Yirmiahu Yovel, *Kant and the Philosophy of History* (Princeton: Princeton University Press, 1980), pp. 114, 215.

7. E.g., *Conflict of the Faculties* VII, 9-10, and *KrV* III and IV, A748-50=B776-8.

2. The "Constitutive" View of Autonomy

With this background in Kant's views about religion and morality, we can now come to his views about autonomy. Here contemporary secular Kantians have produced a line of interpretation which has indeed been alarming to Christian believers who want to say that humans are under the authority of God's command. But here, too, we can be better interpreters of Kant than they are. Kant's view of autonomy, I shall argue, is not a form of creative anti-realism.[8] He is what I will call a "transcendent realist," namely someone who *believes* that there *is* something beyond the limitations of our understanding. In particular there is a God who is head of the kingdom of which we are merely members. But interpreting Kant's view of autonomy as a form of creative anti-realism has been typical of John Rawls and his disciples, and this interpretation has become very influential.

For example, J. B. Schneewind has recently given us a 600-page history of modern ethics leading up to Kant.[9] He lays out, in Kant's

8. I think this is true of his philosophy in general. We need to see three moments in his thought (to use a Hegelian term). He is an empirical realist, a transcendental idealist, but then a transcendent realist. This is a traditional view. See Heinz Heimsoeth, "Metaphysical Motives in the Development of Critical Idealism," in *Kant: Disputed Questions*, ed. M. S. Gram (Chicago: Quadrangle Books, 1967). I have been influenced by Robert M. Adams, "Things in Themselves," *Philosophy and Phenomenological Research* 57, no. 4 (Dec. 1997): 801-25.

9. J. B. Schneewind, *The Invention of Autonomy*. Curiously, the actual treatment of Kant at the end of this volume is brief, almost perfunctory. Schneewind has, however, given a fuller treatment of Kant's views on autonomy in a succession of articles, and I have made use especially of "The Divine Corporation and the History of Ethics," in *Philosophy and History,* ed. Richard Rorty, J. B. Schneewind, and Quentin Skinner (Cambridge: Cambridge University Press, 1984), pp. 173-92; "Natural Law, Skepticism and Methods of Ethics," *Journal of the History of Ideas* 52 (1991): 289-314; and "Autonomy, Obligation and Virtue: An Overview of Kant's Ethics," in *The Cambridge Companion to Kant,* ed. Paul Guyer (Cambridge: Cambridge University Press, 1992), pp. 309-41.

name, what he calls a "constitutive" method of ethics. "Reflecting on one's motives one finds oneself giving them a unique kind of approval or disapproval; in any particular situation one is to act from the approved motive or set of motives, and the act so motivated is the appropriate action. There is no other source of rightness or wrongness in actions."[10] In this passage there are two key differences from the structure that I laid out in the first chapter. There is the motive (or desire) that is a response to a certain kind of situation. But Schneewind does not include under the situation the causal feature that I called "the pull to the good." Then there is the reflective approval or disapproval of one's motives or desires, which is what I called in my first chapter "endorsement." But Schneewind's constitutive method is strikingly different from mine in that he thinks this endorsement is the *source of the rightness* of the action. That is what makes his method "constitutive," or a kind of creative anti-realism. On the view I presented in chapter one, endorsement is indeed a necessary component of moral judgment. But it is not what *makes* an action right, or *constitutes* its rightness. Schneewind goes on to use the language of creation, saying that our possession of a constitutive method of ethics "shows that we *create* the moral order in which we live, and supply our own motives for compliance."[11] The view is that if any other will, or anything external to us, or even our own non-rational appetites are the source of the normativity, then we are not free but slaves.

10. J. B. Schneewind, "Natural Law, Skepticism and Methods of Ethics," p. 298. Similarly Christine Korsgaard takes the view that our reflective endorsement of a prescription makes that prescription normative; it is the source of obligation, or even of all value. See *The Sources of Normativity* (Cambridge: Cambridge University Press, 1996), p. 91; and *Creating the Kingdom of Ends* (Cambridge: Cambridge University Press, 1996), pp. 240-41.

11. J. B. Schneewind, "Natural Law, Skepticism and Methods of Ethics," p. 302, emphasis added. In *The Invention of Autonomy*, Schneewind does not emphasize the language of creation, but he does say that Kant agrees with his predecessors who hold that moral approval is "like the Pufendorfian divine will that creates moral entities," so that "our approval is what makes some motives good, others bad" (p. 524).

This kind of creative anti-realism in ethics is wrong, I think, both in itself and as an interpretation of Kant. I argued against such a view in itself in the first chapter of this book. The best place to see why it does not fit Kant is those passages found throughout Kant's writings where he describes God as the head of the kingdom of which we are mere members, and where he says we should recognize our duties as God's commands to us.[12] But even though they are God's commands, Kant denies that God is the author or creator of the moral demand, because he thinks this demand does not strictly have an *author* at all. But if it does not have an author, then *we* cannot be its author or its creator either. So *creative* anti-realism must be wrong. In his Lectures on Ethics from 1775 to 1780 Kant says that the laws of morality are necessary, like the fact that a triangle has three angles. Only contingent laws, like the law to drive on the right-hand side of the road, can have an author.[13] Necessary laws do not have an author, but they can have someone who promulgates or declares them, and in that sense they are subject to a lawgiver *(unter einem Gesetzgeber stehen)*.

Kant then revises this position in the *Groundwork* (1785), but what looks like a radical revision is not. He says, it is true, that autonomous agents are authors of the law. But this is because he has meanwhile made a distinction not present in the earlier discussion between two kinds of author. Put carefully, it turns out that God and we can both be seen as authors in the one sense, namely authors of the obligation of the law, and neither God nor we can be seen as authors in the other sense, namely authors in the sense of creators.[14] I

12. Strangely, Schneewind does not discuss these passages, as far as I have been able to determine.

13. "There can exist a being which has the power and authority to execute these laws, to declare that they are in accordance with his will, and to impose upon everyone the obligation of acting in accordance with them. This being is therefore the lawgiver, though not the author of the laws," *Lectures on Ethics,* trans. Louis Infield (Indianapolis: Hackett, 1963), pp. 51-52.

14. Kant says that practical reason (the will) should be allowed to "simply

think this is Kant's view at the time of the *Groundwork* and through-out his ethical writing thereafter. Saying that God and we are both authors of the obligation of the law does not mean that we are on an equal footing with God as authors in this sense. It does not mean that our contributions are symmetrical. Kant distinguishes between the head of the moral kingdom to which we belong and the rest of the membership of this kingdom, and says that the head of the king-dom must be a completely independent being, without needs and with an unlimited power adequate to his will.[15] There is no doubt that Kant is talking about God here, as head or king of the kingdom, and without such a king (as we shall see later) there cannot be a king-dom at all. This means that there is the following asymmetry be-tween the king and his subjects: We ordinary moral agents have to

---

manifest its own sovereign authority as the supreme maker of law," and earlier he glosses this notion of the will *making the law* in terms of the will being its *author, Groundwork of the Metaphysics of Morals (Gl)* IV, 441 and 431. Patrick Kain has traced with great elegance the emergence of the new way of making the distinction, in the fifth chapter of his dissertation from the University of No-tre Dame (1999). For example, in the fragment of lecture notes referred to as "Moral Mrongovius II," Kant is reported to have said to his students in 1785 (while he was writing the *Groundwork*), "The lawgiver is not the author of the law, rather he is the author of the obligation of the law *(Autor der obligation des Gezetzes)*," XXIX, 633-34. The new way of stating the distinction becomes standard for him, as in the following passage from the *Metaphysics of Morals* (1797): "A [morally practical] *law* is a proposition that contains a categorical imperative [a command]. One who commands *(imperans)* through a law is the lawgiver *(legislator)*. He is the author *(autor, sic)* of the obligation in accordance with the law *(Urheber [autor] der Verbindlichkeit nach dem Gesetz)*, but not always the author of the law. In the latter case the law would be a positive (contin-gent) and chosen law. A law that binds us a priori and unconditionally by our own reason can also be expressed as proceeding from the will of a supreme lawgiver, that is, one who has only rights and no duties (hence from the divine will); but this signifies only the Idea of a moral being whose will is a law for ev-eryone, without his being thought as the author of the law." Here we have es-sentially the same distinction between lawgiver and author, but now ex-pressed in terms of two kinds of authorship *(MM* VI, 227).

15. *Gl* IV, 433-34.

see our role as recapitulating in our own wills the declaration in God's will of our duties. This is how we are lawgivers; we declare a correspondence of our wills with the law (which we do not create). For me to will the law autonomously is to declare it my law. A good word here is appropriation, which comes from the Latin *ad proprium,* to make one's own. Autonomy on this reading is more nearly a kind of submission than a kind of creation. In what follows, I will use the term "autonomy" with this understanding. But I do not want to deny that the term has been used by others, especially by followers and interpreters of Kant, in a creative anti-realist way.[16]

The constitutive account of Kant has fallen into the trap of a false dichotomy, which I discussed in the first chapter. It is easy, but a mistake, to assume that if values are not entirely independent of or external to the will, they must be entirely dependent on it or internal to it. One way to think of this false dichotomy is to suppose that if values are not like armadillos, things we discover in the world outside us, they must be like armchairs, things we put into the world or create, our artifacts. In the first chapter I was concerned to defend a middle ground that denies both of these exclusive claims.[17] To make a moral judgment is, I claimed, to provide guidance and not merely to report the existence of some perceived (moral) value. It is first-personal and not third-personal. In this sense it is internal, express-

16. See Don Cupitt, *Taking Leave of God* (London: SCM Press, 1980), p. 9: "A modern person must not any more surrender the apex of his self-consciousness to a god. It must remain his own." Kant has language in the Second Critique about willing that there is a God, which sounds at first hearing like blasphemy (*KpV* V, 143). But Kant means that we make God our God. He does not mean "create" in either case, either that we create the law or that we create God. Neither God nor the law can do the job Kant needs them to do if we do create them.

17. I am encouraged in my diagnosis by Karl Ameriks, whose interpretation of Kant ("On Schneewind and Kant's Method in Ethics," *Ideas y Valores* 102 [December 1996]: 48) "eschews the false dichotomy of 'either imposed by us or imposed by another,' . . . or the false trichotomy: either imposed by us, or imposed by another, or simply 'perceived' as a natural feature."

ing a commitment of the will. But this does not mean that it is not accountable to independent standards, or that such standards derive merely from our own will. Kant's theory is, I believe, a good example of a theory that resists the dichotomy.[18]

3. Christian August Crusius

An important figure for us to consider here is Christian August Crusius.[19] Kant needs to be understood (and has not usually been understood) against the background of the discussion of divine command theory in the pietist circles he was familiar with. Crusius was influential in Königsberg at the time Kant was writing the *Groundwork,* and provided a pietist alternative within philosophy to the rationalist doctrine of Christian Wolff. This was a war, between pietism and rationalism, which is a recurrent tension in the Christian church. August Hermann Francke, the leader of the pietists,

---

18. This coincidence is not accidental. For it is Kant whom Austin claims as the ancestor of the rejection of "the descriptive fallacy," as I described in the first chapter, and this rejection lies behind the middle-ground or "prescriptive realist" position I was defending in that chapter. The mistake Austin identified lies behind the position of Korsgaard and Schneewind, who think they have to move from a rejection of substantive moral realism to a *creative* anti-realism.

19. Paton already remarked on this importance. See Immanuel Kant, *Groundwork of the Metaphysics of Morals,* trans. and analyzed by H. J. Paton (New York: Harper, 1964), p. 141. For Crusius's views, see the selection from "Guide to Rational Living," in *Moral Philosophy from Montaigne to Kant,* vol. 2, ed. J. B. Schneewind (Cambridge: Cambridge University Press, 1990), pp. 568-85 (henceforth *GRL*). See also Giorgio Tonelli, "La question des bornes de l'entendement humain au XVIIIe siècle," *Revue de Métaphysique et de Morale* (1959): 396-427. In the Second Critique (*KpV*, 40), Kant mentions Crusius as the source of the view which locates the practical material determining the ground of morality externally in the will of God. See also *Moralphilosophie Collins, KGS,* pp. 262-63: "Crusius believes that all obligation is related to the will of another *(die Willkür eines andern).*"

complained to the king (Frederick William I) that Wolff, the rationalist, was teaching a heretical notion of common grace, that Confu-
cius had adequate knowledge of God and had discovered all the important truths about morality without any knowledge of Christ or
Christianity. The king then stopped Wolff teaching philosophy and
banished him from the kingdom (though he was allowed to return
under the next king, Frederick the Great, in 1740). Kant's teacher,
Martin Knutzen, undertook the project of seeing if the pietism of
Crusius and the rationalism of Wolff could be reconciled.

Schneewind's magisterial history of ethics, which I referred to
earlier, presents Crusius as making two central points against
Wolff's moral philosophy. First, Crusius introduced what Schneewind calls "a quite novel distinction" between two kinds of things we
ought to do: there are actions that we ought to do as *means* to some
end of ours and others we ought to do *regardless* of any ends we have,
even the end of our own perfection. It is only this second kind of obligation that Crusius is willing to call "moral obligation." Here, says
Schneewind, is the origin of Kant's notion of the categorical imperative. Second, Crusius tied this distinction to the notion of freedom.
He said that the will is free only because it can choose in accordance
with this second kind of obligation, regardless of our ends. That is to
say that even if we perceive something clearly as required for an increase in perfection, we can choose either for it or against it. This is
contrary to Wolff because Wolff taught that by nature the availabil-
ity of increased perfection necessarily moves us, and we are always
obligated to pursue it. We are always drawn to act so as to bring
about what we believe is the greatest amount of perfection, and
Wolff says we are bound or necessitated so to act.[20]

But have we not met these two points of Crusius before? Is it
really, as Schneewind says, "a quite novel distinction" to distinguish
being drawn to some end of ours *as ours* and being drawn *regardless* of
any ends we have, even the end of our own perfection? Have we not

20. J. B. Schneewind, "Autonomy, Obligation and Virtue," pp. 312-13.

met the distinctive tying of this distinction to freedom? Duns Scotus holds that there are two affections of the will, the affection for advantage, directed to one's own happiness or perfection, and the affection for justice, which is directed to what is good in itself regardless of one's ends. And tying this distinction to the nature of freedom is also characteristic of Scotus. I do not mean to imply that Crusius got the distinction from Scotus. As I said in the second chapter, Scotism was a widely accessible option in the intellectual milieu in which the Reformers lived.[21] Luther makes the point repeatedly that one who does the good in order to promote his own blessedness is still not devoted to the good itself; rather, he is using it as a means for "climbing up to the Divine majesty."[22] No doubt Crusius came to the distinction by reflecting on Luther.

In Scotus and in the Reformers and in Crusius, this distinction is tied into a version of divine command theory. Scotus thinks that God necessarily loves God, and then wills to have co-lovers (though God does not will this necessarily). Moreover God necessarily orders these creatures towards himself, the primary good. From this come the commandments of the first table of the Decalogue. But what I called in the previous chapter the *route* to this end is not necessary, and is within God's prescriptive discretion. I gave the picture of the mother setting up a treasure hunt. Here we have the second table of the law, which is binding upon us because God has chosen it;

---

21. For Luther, the route is through Ockham. The nominalist tradition or *via moderna* was adopted by Gregory of Rimini, who was General of the Hermits of St. Augustine, which was Luther's order a century and a half later. Gabriel Biel, at Tübingen, wrote an influential exposition of Ockham's system, which was taught at Erfurt (by two of Luther's professors, Jaadokus Trutfetter and Bartholomaeus Arnoldi) and at Wittenberg (where Luther did most of his teaching). See especially Heiko Oberman, *Luther: A Man Between God and the Devil,* trans. Eileen Walliser-Schwarzenbart (New York: Doubleday, 1989), pp. 118-19.

22. *WA* 2, 493, 12ff. See also *WA* 37, 662, 18ff. This theme is taken to its limit by Anders Nygren, in *Agape and Eros,* trans. Philip S. Watson (New York: Harper and Row, 1969), e.g., pp. 701f.

though it is not arbitrary, because it leads to our final end. Now Schneewind, like Socrates in the *Euthyphro,* presents us with a dichotomy: "whether morally right acts are right simply because God commands us to do them, or whether, by contrast, God commands us to do them because they are, in themselves, right."[23] But the Scotist form of divine command theory does not fit this dichotomy. Our duties to our neighbor are right both because God chooses that route and because it is a route to the final good. In Crusius there is the same kind of structure as in Scotus. God has an essential tendency to self-affirmation, and when God creates us (which is not necessary) God *must* desire that our strivings should be directed in accordance with our highest objective end, and so towards God. But this means, Crusius says, that our highest formal end is compliance with God's will and command.[24]

Crusius does not merely recapitulate Scotus, however; he adds to him. I want to emphasize one such addition, and I want to claim that this addition is the focus of Kant's objection in the famous argument in the *Groundwork.* The addition is most clearly seen in the way Crusius divides up the basic human desires. Scotus was concerned to deny eudaimonism, the view that all our motivation is directed towards happiness. He therefore divided up the affection for advantage and the affection for justice. Crusius is likewise opposed to eudaimonism. But for him there are not two but three basic drives. The first is the drive to increase *our own* appropriate perfection, and from this come the desires for truth, clarity, good reasoning, the arts, bodily improvement, freedom, friendship, and honor. Second comes the *disinterested* or impartial drive for perfection, and from this comes a general desire to help others. But third, and distinct and incommensurable with these first two, is what Crusius calls "the drive of conscience," which is "the natural drive to recog-

23. Schneewind, "The Divine Corporation and the History of Ethics," p. 176.
24. *GRL* 176 and 216.

nize *a divine moral law*." His idea is that we have within us this separate capacity to recognize divine command and to be drawn towards
it out of a sense of dependence on the God who prescribes the command to us, and will punish us if we disobey (*GRL* 132). It is a good
thing, Crusius thinks, that we do have this drive of conscience. For
there is no way that most of us could most of the time reason out
what we ought to do. God therefore gives us a "shorter path" to
knowledge of the divine law, and makes the divine will evident in
such a way that it can come to everyone's knowledge (*GRL* 135). In
this way, no one is excused from accountability.

Crusius is proposing a human capacity for receiving divine command as such, and he separates this from the mere disinterested desire for perfection (or what Scotus would call the affection for justice). He is not talking about the reception of divine command on
special occasions, but a general human capacity; this is why he
thinks it helps with the accountability problem. He is giving a particular reading of Romans 1 and 2, in which the law is written "on our
hearts" and even those who "suppress the truth" are "without ex-
cuse." This drive of conscience is supposed to be a sense which humans quite generally have of being dependent on some other being
and therefore of having obligation to do what that other being tells
them to do. But recognizing the commands of this being and being
moved to obey is supposed to be different from recognizing intrinsic
good and being moved to pursue it.

Schneewind has the wrong distinction between Kant and
Crusius. Schneewind thinks *Kant* is trying to show how we as moral
agents can be independent of divine legislation, and how morality
can be a human creation. Schneewind takes *Crusius,* on the other
hand, to be arguing that we are dependent on God. Here is Schneewind's dichotomy. Either there is *independence* of obligation from
God, as in Kant, or there is a wormlike *dependence,* as in Crusius. I am
going to show that Kant's actual view is neither of these, and that we
should follow Kant in this respect.

4. Kant's Argument about
Divine Commands in the *Groundwork*

Now we can go to the brief (and famous) argument in the *Ground-work* which is often taken to be an argument against divine command theory in general. Since Kant's argument is brief, I will quote it in full. Kant rejects "the theological concept which derives morality from a divine and supremely perfect will; not merely because we cannot intuit God's perfection and can only derive it from our own concepts, among which that of morality is the most eminent; but because, if we do not do this (and to do so would be to give a crudely circular explanation), the concept of God's will still remaining to us — one drawn from such characteristics as lust for glory and domination and bound up with frightful ideas of power and vengefulness — would inevitably form the basis for a moral system which would be in direct opposition to morality."[25]

The typical reading of this argument in twentieth-century analytic philosophy takes it as a refutation of the divine command theory of ethical obligation in general. Here, to give just one prominent example, is R. M. Hare's verdict: "Ever since Kant, it has been *possible* for people to insist on the autonomy of morals — its independence of human or divine authority. Indeed, it has been *necessary*, if they were to think morally, in the sense in which that word is now generally understood."[26] The claim here is that Kant has made it possible for us to think of morality as independent of divine or human authority, and that we now have to think of it that way if we want to use the moral words in the way most people understand them.[27]

---

25. *Gl* IV, 443.

26. R. M. Hare in "The Simple Believer," reprinted in *Essays on Religion and Education* (Oxford: Clarendon Press, 1992), p. 30. See also *Sorting Out Ethics* (Oxford: Clarendon Press, 1997), p. 27. This argument in the *Groundwork* has had the same kind of status in Ethics as the treatment of the Ontological Argument in the First Critique has had in Metaphysics.

27. The empirical claim here that the word usage of most people in the

Similarly, Lewis White Beck takes Kant to be arguing that moral duties do not owe their authority in any way to being divine commands. After conceding that Kant talks *as if* he were a divine command theorist (in this sense), Beck says on Kant's behalf, "It is not that [duties] *are* divine commands, or that they owe their authority over us to their being decrees of a divine lawgiver who also created us; for in that event, we should have to know about God before we could know what our duty is, and we do not know God, while even the most unphilosophical person knows his duty. Moreover, such a theory would be incompatible with moral self-government, or autonomy."[28] So Beck interprets Kant as saying that we should regard the moral law *as if* it were a divine command, and the people under this law *as if* it were "a people united by common allegiance to a *supposed* author of these commands, namely God."[29] But the "as if" in these contexts is stressed in such a way as to deny that we should believe in the actual existence of such divine commands or their legisla-

---

world has divorced morality and divine command is highly dubious. Maybe this is true of most professional philosophers. Other examples of the kind of interpretation I am objecting to are A. C. Ewing, *Value and Reality* (London: Allen and Unwin, 1973), pp. 183-87, and James Rachels, "God and Human Attitudes," reprinted in *Divine Commands and Morality,* ed. Paul Helm (Oxford: Oxford University Press, 1981), pp. 34-48, especially 44f. One vivid example I quoted in the first chapter is from Iris Murdoch, *The Sovereignty of Good* (New York: Schocken Books, 1971), p. 80: "Kant's man had already nearly a century earlier received a glorious incarnation in the work of Milton: his proper name is Lucifer." The argument itself, without explicit attachment to Kant, is pervasive. One nice statement of it is in P. H. Nowell-Smith's *Ethics* (Harmondsworth: Penguin Books, 1954), pp. 192-93.

28. Lewis White Beck, *Six Secular Philosophers* (New York: Harper, 1960), p. 72. But it is not in general true for Kant that a prescription has authority only if we know about its source. As I shall argue, Kant thinks that the prescriptions of a legitimate political ruler have authority and have their source in his will; but we do not have knowledge about this will.

29. Beck, *Six Secular Philosophers*, p. 74 (emphasis added). See also R. M. Hare, *Sorting Out Ethics,* p. 27: "God, whom Kant would have liked to believe in."

tor. God's existence is not, however, for Kant, "as if."[30] Kant is not an agnostic, except that he does not "know" in his own very restricted sense of "knowing," according to which we can only know what we could possibly experience with the senses. We could not experience God this way, and so we do not in this sense know that God exists. But Kant holds that we are required to *believe* that God exists. In just the same sense, he holds that we are required to believe that God is (with us) the legislator of moral law, and (unlike us) the rewarder and punisher of our lives as a whole in relation to this law. We have to deny knowledge, he says, in order to make room for faith.

If, like most contemporary exegetes, one reads Kant's argument as an attack on divine command theory in general, it will naturally be construed as presenting the following two-horned dilemma. We have two choices on the divine command theory: Either we derive the notion of God's perfection from our moral concepts or we do not. If we do (the first horn), then the derivation which the divine command theory proposes is crudely circular. It says we have moral obligations because God commands them, and we should obey God's commands because they are morally right. But if we separate (on the second horn) our notion of God's will from the moral concepts, then the explanation of our obligation will depend merely on our ability to please God and God's ability (if we do not) to hurt us. The relationship between us, when stripped of right, will reduce to one of power. But then morality will be based on self-interest, and will not be what (on Kant's view) morality in fact is. So neither choice is available to us, and so the divine command theory should be rejected.[31]

---

30. Kant does use the "as if" locution counterfactually, but to express what our moral lives would be like *without* God: "each must, on the contrary, so conduct himself as if everything depended on him" (*Rel.* VI, 101).

31. There are problems with the argument on this second horn. What needs to be attended to is the *different* ways in which we can separate God's will from the moral concepts. On God's side we can distinguish the claim that the divine will is inconsistent with what is morally right from the claim that

This is an important argument, and I will come back to it at the end. But it cannot be, if Kant is consistent, Kant's argument. For Kant accepts the view throughout his life that we should recognize our obligations as God's commands. For example, there is the passage in *Lectures on Ethics:* "Our bearing towards God must be characterized by reverence, love and fear — reverence for Him as a holy lawgiver, love for His beneficent rule, and fear of Him as a just judge" (which is different, Kant says, from merely being afraid of God when we have transgressed). "We show our reverence by regarding His law as holy and righteous, by due respect for it, and by seeking to fulfil it in our disposition."[32] I have already mentioned the passage in the *Groundwork* about God as the head of the kingdom of ends, and the passages in the Second Critique and *Religion within the Limits of Reason Alone* about recognizing our duties as God's commands. Because this is a sustained theme in Kant, we are better off regarding his attack in the *Groundwork* as directed at some more specific target. The theory of Crusius is an excellent candidate.[33]

Kant objects to Crusius's theory on three grounds. He starts the argument by saying that we cannot intuit God's perfection. This starting point makes sense if it is Crusius he has in mind. Crusius had proposed that we have a separate access to divine perfection through "the drive of conscience," separate from the general moral love or the disinterested drive for perfection.[34] Kant's position is, rather, that we cannot intuit God's perfection, because human intu-

---

this willing, though consistent, does not go through the moral concepts. On our side we can distinguish the claim that we have to obey even if God's will is inconsistent with what is morally right from the claim that we must obey even in cases where we cannot determine whether God's will is consistent with what is morally right or not.

32. Kant, *Lectures on Ethics*, p. 97.

33. Crusius also took the position on the authority of Scripture that no rational criticism of the Bible was permitted, and that its meaning could be penetrated only by a kind of empathy or inner light. Kant objects to this claim as well, but not in the same argument.

34. *GRL* 132.

ition is limited within space and time. This is his first objection. Our access is, therefore, through concepts. Either these will be the moral concepts, or some other. This presents a Crusius-type divine command theory with a dilemma.

Suppose we take the first option, and reply that we *can* know what God wills, since he wills what the moral law prescribes. Here is the second objection. This would be, Kant says, *crudely* circular. He may be objecting to just such a crude circle in the passage from Crusius I quoted earlier: "Finally, the third of the basic human drives is the natural drive to recognize a divine *moral* law" (*GRL* 132, emphasis added).[35] Crusius adds the word "moral" at a key point in his definition without showing how he can simultaneously insist on the separation of the three basic drives.[36] It is a crude circle to prove that A is B by adding B to the definition of A. What is needed is a "third term," C, which can be connected first with A and then with B.[37] In Kant's own account the third term is provided by our membership with God in the kingdom of ends. But Crusius just gives us the crude circle without such mediation.

35. *GRL* 132, emphasis added. See Lewis White Beck, *A Commentary on Kant's Critique of Practical Reason* (Chicago: University of Chicago Press, 1960), p. 107: "Either Crusius surreptitiously introduces ethical predicates into the concept of divine perfection [and Beck refers to this passage of Crusius], with the result that theological perfection no longer grounds the moral principle but presupposes it; or a hedonistic motivation is postulated as the ground of obedience to God." But Kant is not exactly accusing Crusius of this second error, as I will argue in the following paragraph.

36. "It is thus not specially necessary to show that the drive of conscience is distinct from the previously distinguished basic drives, as its object is so very different from those of the other drives" (*GRL* 134).

37. An instructive comparison is Kant's fear in the third section of *Groundwork* that he may have argued in a circle about morality and freedom (*Gl* IV, 450). Kant thinks he has extricated himself from the viciousness of this circle when he later points out that "when we think of ourselves as free, we transfer ourselves into the intelligible world as members" (*Gl* IV, 453). He gives us here a third term which mediates between morality and freedom, namely our membership in the intelligible world.

106

Finally, Kant makes a third point against Crusius. If we think we can understand what God is telling us to do *without* using the moral concepts, we will be left without morality at all. Kant's target must be a form of the divine command theory which forbids us to say that we should obey God because God cares for our happiness and perfection. In other words, we are forbidden by this form of the theory to appeal to what Kant calls practical love. A Crusius-type divine command theory insists that we should obey God's will *just* because it is God's will, *whatever* our direct intuition tells us that will is.[38] This makes a nonsense of morality. The point of morality, as Kant sees it, is to further one's own perfection and the happiness of others.[39] The kingdom of ends is the place where these two goals coincide. A morality that ignored one's own perfection and the happiness of others would be unintelligible. But this is just the kind of morality Crusius seems to be asking us to adopt as our own. It is not that Crusius is here making the gross claim that what should move us to obedience is hope of reward or fear of punishment. Indeed, I started from his insistence, which he holds in common with Scotus, that we have sources of motivation other than our own happiness or perfection. It is notable that Kant also, in his reply, does not say that his opponent bases morality on hope of reward or fear of punishment, but rather "that the concept of God's will remaining to us," if we separate out the drive of conscience from the disinterested desire to help other people, will be drawn from

38. See Robert M. Adams, "Autonomy and Theological Ethics," in *The Virtue of Faith* (Oxford: Oxford University Press, 1987), pp. 123-27. Adams approves of Tillich's notion of theonomous ethics: "The theonomous agent acts morally because he loves God, but also because he loves what God loves." Kant on my reading, but not Crusius, has a theonomous ethics. I will return to Adams at the end of this chapter. Crusius himself would not be worried by this objection. See Tonelli, "La question des bornes," p. 410 (my translation): "Crusius underlines the importance of *mysteries of reason,* mainly theological doctrines which have to be admitted, even though we do not understand how certain things can be joined together or separated in such a way."

39. This is to put the point in terms of the *matter* of morality, rather than its form (which is more usual in the *Groundwork*). See the *MM* VI, 398.

"such characteristics as lust for glory and domination and bound up with frightful ideas of power and vengefulness." Kant is interested in what our idea of God will be like if we make the separation of the drive of conscience that Crusius suggests. And we find that Crusius does emphasize that it is a God who will punish us if we do not obey, even though this is not to be our motivation for obedience.[40] It would have been easy for Kant, if he were making a general attack on divine command theory, to make the point about not basing morality on fear or hope of reward, and I suspect that is the way his argument is in fact usually taught. I used to teach it that way myself. But it is not what Kant says. So all three steps of the argument are specifically tailored to attack Crusius.

Is Kant taking us back in this argument to a pre-Crusian Scotist form of divine command theory? In some ways, yes. Kant shares with Scotus the view that there are the two basic affections of the will, and that we start with the wrongful ranking of them. He shares the view that our freedom is tied to the good will. Two major differences are that Kant makes no distinction in terms of necessity and contingency between the first and second tables of the law. And he describes our final end not as being co-lovers with God, but as a perfect combination of virtue and happiness. But I want to stress two similarities. In both Scotus and Kant, we share our final end with God, in the sense that we and God both aim at what is best for us. And in both Scotus and Kant God is constrained here by necessity, despite Scotus's emphasis on God's choosing of the second table.[41] I will return to these points at the end of the chapter.

---

40. "The motive of conscience," he says, "is therefore merely a motive to recognize certain indebtednesses, that is, such universal obligations as one must observe *even if one does not wish to consider the advantages and disadvantages deriving from them,* whose transgression God *will punish* and, if his law is not to be in vain, *must punish*" (*GRL* 133, emphasis added).

41. In the *Lectures on Ethics* (p. 22), Kant is reported to have distinguished between positive (or contingent) obligation and natural obligation, which arises from the nature of the action itself; and then to have complained,

5. Autonomous Relations to Political Authority

We can see that Kant thinks submission is compatible with autonomy if we compare what he says our relation is to *political* authority.
Kant believes that autonomy is not only consistent with submission
to political authority, but requires this submission. His argument is
that coercion by the state is necessary in order to prevent coercion by
individuals, which would be an obstacle to the external exercise of
autonomy. External compulsion by the state is thus "a hindering of
the hindrances to freedom."[42] This is laid out nicely in the following
passage from Mary Gregor's introduction to the *Metaphysics of
Morals:* "It is only within a civil condition, where there is a legislator
to enact laws, an executive to enforce them, and a judiciary to settle
disputes about rights by reference to such public laws, that human
beings can do what it can be known a priori they must be able to do
in accordance with moral principles."[43] The justification of the state
then rests for Kant on moral grounds, on the freedom of each individual person and our obligation to respect this in each other. A citizen is in this way morally justified in adopting into her own will the
will of her ruler. The analogy with God's rule is systematic. Kant

---

"Crusius believes that all obligation is related to the will of another. So in his
view all obligation would be a necessitation *per arbitrium alterius.* It may indeed
seem that in an obligation we are necessitated *per arbitrium alterius;* but in fact
I am necessitated by an *arbitrium internum,* not *externum,* and thus by the necessary condition of universal will." On my view, Kant is objecting not to the
appeal to a superior will, but to making this will merely external, or separate
from the universal will. In Kant's own way of recognizing our duties as God's
commands, this can be and should be consistent with seeing them as permitted by the moral law, and thus the universal will. To put this more simply,
what Kant wants in our autonomous submission is both our will and God's
together, neither of them being sufficient without the other.

42. *MM* VI, 396. See also *MM* VI, 231: "[Whatever] counteracts the hin-
drance of an effect promotes that effect and is consistent with it."

43. Mary Gregor, translator's introduction to *The Metaphysics of Morals*
(Cambridge: Cambridge University Press, 1991), p. 10.

gives God executive and judicial as well as legislative functions within the kingdom, and God has to exercise those functions in order for the subjects of this kingdom to exercise the freedom that morality gives them. The analogy in fact goes beyond this, though I will not spell this out. Just as in God's kingdom, so in an earthly kingdom there are three kinds of mistakes a citizen might be making in claiming justification for her obedience. They are the same three kinds of mistakes Crusius makes in analyzing our relation to God. The point I want to make here, though, is that Kant cannot mean to construct an argument from autonomy against all forms of external authority. The opposite is true. He thinks that autonomy requires submission to at least one kind of external authority, namely the authority of the state.

The analogy with political authority is helpful in understanding the role of sanctions in our relation to God. God can punish and reward us. As we have already seen, this is not supposed to be the *ground* of our obedience. But it is essentially tied to the way in which God can be the author of the *obligation* to obey the law in a way that we are not. Consider the example of a student who takes a logic course because it is required by his department.[44] It might seem that he acts more autonomously if he takes it because he independently sees its merit. But he acts autonomously out of his practical identity *as a student* only if he places the right to make and enforce some of the decisions about what he will study in the hands of his teachers. Similarly, a good citizen *as a citizen* does not pay her taxes because she thinks the government needs the money. She can *vote* for taxes for that reason. But once the vote is over, she must pay her taxes because it is the law. To extend this analysis to the context of divine command theory, we could say that an agent acts autonomously out

44. Korsgaard, *The Sources of Normativity*, pp. 25f. and 105-7. She goes on to argue against Hobbes and Pufendorf that our moral obligations have authority because of the *internal* sanction of a painful conscience. But Kant, I am arguing, preserves the need for an external imposition of sanctions, though they are not arbitrary (*KpV* V, 130).

of her practical identity as a citizen of the kingdom of which God is head only if she acts out of obedience to God. In none of these three cases (the student, the citizen of an earthly kingdom, and the citizen of God's kingdom) is there any inconsistency with the agent sharing the ends of her superior. But in all three cases there is a true duty "which must be represented as *at the same time* that [superior's] command."[45] The role of the sanctions is to make the kingdom possible, and the ground of obedience is not fear of the sanctions but membership in the kingdom.

It is worth spelling out why the kingdom of ends has to be a *kingdom* and not, for example, a republic.[46] Korsgaard glosses the kingdom of ends as "the republic of all rational beings," and she also calls a friendship "a kingdom of two."[47] J. L. Mackie is more accurate here. He says, "But for the need to give God a special place in it [the kingdom of ends] would have been better called a commonwealth of ends."[48] In Kant's theory God has combined in one person, in his kingdom, the legislative, executive, and judicial functions that Kant thinks should be separated in a well-run earthly republic. In brief, "We must conceive a Supreme Being whose laws are holy, whose government is benevolent and whose rewards and punishments are just."[49]

The *legislative* function we have already met. But there is a key difference from the legislation of an earthly state. Ethical legislation concerns the heart, and not merely the behavior of the citizenry. Kant accordingly says that the ruler of the ethical realm

45. *Rel.* VI, 99.

46. For Kant's republican sympathies, see *MM* VI, 40-42. Note R. M. Hare, *Sorting Out Ethics,* p. 26: "The Kingdom of Ends is not really a kingdom, but a democracy with equality before the law." It is hard for our contemporaries, especially for Americans, to think in terms of a morally legitimate king. Perhaps a weak analogy would be a kindergarten teacher who combines legislative, executive, and judicial functions without thereby being a tyrant.

47. Korsgaard, *The Sources of Normativity,* pp. 99 and 127.

48. J. L. Mackie, *Ethics* (Harmondsworth: Penguin, 1977), p. 45.

49. *Lectures on Ethics,* pp. 79-80.

"must be one who knows the heart, in order to penetrate to the most intimate parts of the disposition of each and everyone and, as must be in every community, give to each according to the worth of his actions." God's promulgating the moral law to the heart is what Kant describes in the preface to the second edition of *Religion* as the revelation to reason. There is an additional point here. God, as legislator, will not ask us to do what is impossible for us, though we may be asked to do what is impossible for us on our own. The point is that God offers us the assistance to do what God calls us to do.

God's *executive* function can be divided into various parts. One part is the execution of the rewards and punishments that God declares in his judicial function. There is also, however, the "maintenance" of the law.[50] We have to believe that a system is in place and is being maintained in which the ends of the other members of the kingdom are consistent with each other and with ours. This is what we might call a coordination problem. The world might be the kind of place in which I can be happy only if other people are not, or in which some of the people I affect by my actions can be happy only if other people I affect are not. I am, as a creature of need, bound to desire my own happiness in everything else I desire (though my happiness is not the only source of my motivation).[51] And I am required to pursue the happiness of others as much as my own.[52] We ought to share each other's ends as far as the moral law allows. This is the content Kant gives to "treating humanity, whether in your own person or in the person of another, always at the same time as an end and

---

50. *Lectures on Ethics,* p. 81.

51. *KpV* V, 25. There is an apparent difficulty here about whether Kant's argument is consistent. I have tried to lay out the argument in *The Moral Gap,* pp. 69-96. Kant wants to say both that we inevitably desire our own happiness and that this desire should be subordinated to duty, which has (as in Crusius) a separate spring of motivation.

52. This is one of the two ingredients in the *matter* of morality described in the *Metaphysics of Morals* (VI, 385-86).

never simply as a means."[53] But we can do all this only if there is a system in place in which others' ends are first consistent with each other and second consistent with our own happiness.[54] Since we do not know the contents either of our own happiness or that of others, we cannot see by inspection whether these consistencies obtain.[55] We need to presuppose, Kant says, the idea of a higher moral being, "through whose universal organization the forces of single individuals, insufficient on their own, are united for a common effect."[56] The common effect Kant has in mind here is the highest good, in which all are virtuous and all are happy. This is his translation of the psalmist's idea of righteousness and peace embracing each other.[57] Kant's point is that we have to believe in God's executive functions in order to have the faith that such a good is possible. In fact, with this belief we can have not merely moral faith but moral hope, because God as Lord of history is bringing the kingdom to fruition.[58]

Finally, the *judicial* function is already implicit in what I have said. We have to suppose that God can see our hearts and can justly separate the sheep and the goats, those who have been obedient and those who have not. It is not merely that God applies justly the standards, but that the standards God applies are just. I will sum up by quoting from the Second Critique, in which Kant stresses that moral rightness is an end common to us and to God, but that God's role as different and non-symmetrical with ours is nonetheless essential to our moral life. "Religion," Kant says, "is the recognition of all duties as divine commands, not as sanctions, i.e., arbitrary and contingent

53. *Gl* IV, 429.

54. If one holds, like Thomas Reid, that there are many self-evident but logically independent moral axioms, then God is required to ensure *their* consistency.

55. *KpV* V, 36.

56. *Rel.* VI, 98.

57. Psalm 85:10.

58. Kant says that the kingdom of heaven is represented "not only as being brought ever nearer in an approach delayed at certain times yet never wholly interrupted, but also as arriving" (*Rel.* VI, 134).

ordinances of a foreign will, but as essential laws of any free will as such. *Even as such,* they must be regarded as commands of the Supreme Being, because we can hope for the highest good (to strive for which is our duty under moral law) only from a morally perfect (holy and beneficent) and omnipotent will; and, therefore, we can hope to attain it only through harmony with this will."[59]

6. Conclusion

I have tried to show that Kant does not intend a general argument against divine command theory. I want to end by showing that the general argument usually but wrongly associated with him does not work. We can see this if we hold onto Kant's and Scotus's view that we and God are jointly but non-symmetrically engaged in our moral life, and that we share our membership in the kingdom with God. Autonomous submission, I want to say, is recapitulating in our wills what God has willed for our willing. This kind of mutuality is present, I think, in the idea of covenant, because a covenant is between people who share commitment to the kind of life the covenant sets up as normative. This allows us to endorse a divine command theory which is what Robert Adams calls "theonomous."[60] Adams says, "Let

---

59. *KpV* V, 130; emphasis added.

60. Adams takes the term "theonomy" from Tillich in the article already referred to. There are also two important papers, "A Modified Divine Command Theory of Ethical Wrongness" and "Divine Command Metaethics Modified Again," both of which are reprinted (the second only in part) in Helm, *Divine Commands and Morality.* My agreement with Adams here does not extend to his treatment of the Abraham and Isaac story in *Finite and Infinite Goods* (Oxford: Oxford University Press, 1998), pp. 277-91. See also Baruch A. Brody, "Morality and Religion Reconsidered," *Readings in the Philosophy of Religion,* ed. Baruch A. Brody (Englewood Cliffs, N.J.: Prentice-Hall, 1974), pp. 592-603, and Philip L. Quinn, *Divine Commands and Moral Requirements* (Oxford: Clarendon Press, 1978). I am not claiming that any of these authors agrees with me in my attribution of a particular kind of divine command theory to Kant.

us say that a person is *theonomous* to the extent that the following is true of him: He regards his moral principles as given him by God, and adheres to them partly out of love or loyalty to God, but he also prizes them for their own sakes, so that they are the principles he *would* give himself if he were giving himself a moral law. The theonomous agent, in so far as he is right, acts morally because he loves God, but also because he loves what God loves."[61]

I want to connect this idea of theonomy with the Scotist distinction between our final end of union with God and our route to that end. The key idea is that the second table of the law, the specification of our duties to the neighbor, is binding on us because God has selected it. Contrary to some versions of natural law theory, this part of the law is not deducible from our human nature. God could have chosen a different route for beings with our nature to reach our final end. I am not attributing this view to Kant. But I am suggesting that, supposing Scotus is right about this, autonomy can be reconciled with a version of divine command theory. If we try to mount the argument from autonomy that is usually (but wrongly) associated with Kant, we will fail. This is because there is nothing heteronomous about willing to obey a superior's prescription because the superior has prescribed it, in a discretionary way, as long as the final end is shared between us, and we have trust also about the route. The dichotomy which the usual version of the argument relies upon is false. The dichotomy is: either our own wills entirely or entirely the will of another. What human moral life is actually like on the Scotist picture is a complex and rich mixture.

The notion of recapitulating God's will in ours is, however, vague in various ways. There is a range of cases here. Willing is always under a description, and the descriptions under which two people share an end may vary.[62] We can go back to the example I discussed

61. Adams, "Autonomy and Theological Ethics." Autonomous submission to political authority ("fredonomy"?) has the same structure.

62. Scotus says, *nihil volitum quin praecognitum* (nothing is willed but what is pre-cognized), *Opus Oxon.* II, dist. 25, q.un.n.19.

in the first chapter of a teenager's mother who prefers that her son not sleep with his girlfriend, but live a fully chaste life by Christian standards for the spiritual union properly surrounding sexual intercourse. Suppose her son does not share her Christian understanding. There is a range of possible ways in which the son might nonetheless repeat his mother's will. Perhaps he does not want to lose his inheritance. This would not be autonomy at all, because it would be a merely prudential judgment. Perhaps he respects his mother, though not her view. He does not want to hurt her, and he is grateful to her. So he does what she says. This is not quite sharing her end, but it is getting closer. Or perhaps he does accept the Christian teaching about sexuality, but barely understands it. He abstains because he wants to be a good Christian, but the commandment makes no sense to him. Here the mother and the son may even share a description under which something is willed, but it is not equally resonant for the two. Finally, the son may share his mother's understanding as well as her prescription. But perhaps this kind of shared understanding is one we can *never* have completely with God, even in heaven. It is possible, then, to share ends with another person, or with God, with many different degrees of clarity and fullness.

I would like to give an example from my own life, and I hope the reader will not think me self-inflating. When I was invited to apply for a job at Calvin College, it did not make rational sense to me to come. I was happy where I was at Lehigh, and the invitation meant giving up tenure (a precious commodity), taking a salary cut, and leaving my sister and her family and all of my wife's family in the East. Moreover, I knew very little indeed about Calvin or the Christian Reformed Church, with which Calvin is affiliated. Nonetheless I felt a sense of call from God that I should accept the invitation. The correspondence from Calvin came on letterhead with the emblem "I offer my heart to thee, Lord, promptly and sincerely," and I felt a conviction that for me offering my heart meant applying to Calvin. I think at this stage my sharing an end with God, if that is what I was doing, was comparatively unclear and tentative. I did not know why

God was asking me to do this, but I trusted that God had my interests at heart as well as those whom I might affect by my teaching and scholarship. Here is the coordination feature I mentioned in connection with God's executive function. It is only afterwards that I have begun to understand and share some of the reasons why this was the right move. Now was my response autonomous or not?

For Schneewind, the answer is that it was not. He constructs a picture of what he calls "the Divine Corporation."[63] He imagines a large corporation, the sort of corporation in which Dilbert finds himself employed. The ordinary employees understand very little about each other's jobs or the purposes of the whole corporation, there is a strong back-up system so that failures by others will be remedied and ordinary employees do not have to feel responsible for the remedy themselves, and the supervisor has made it clear that they are paid for carrying out their duties strictly, "looking neither to left nor to right." This, he says, is the traditional Christian picture of the kingdom of God, with God as the head of the firm. Schneewind thinks progress towards autonomy occurs in the history of ethics as each of these three conditions weakens. First, we come to see the purpose of the "corporation" as promoting human happiness. Second, we see ourselves as the major instruments in producing this end or failing to produce it. Third, we see ourselves as cooperating with each other in producing this end, and as responsible for repairing each other's omissions. In summary, "As God's supervision and activity lessen, man's responsibility increases." I do not want to deny that this movement of thought has occurred within academic philosophy in the last two hundred years. But as far as I can see, there is no way to determine whether this movement is progress towards a desirable kind of autonomy without settling first whether there is a God who has created us and rules the world providentially in the way the traditional picture and Kant himself suggest. If there is, and we decline to regard ourselves as God's subjects, this is not a desirable

63. Schneewind, "The Divine Corporation and the History of Ethics."

form of autonomy but a form of foolishness. It would be like the graduate student in Korsgaard's example refusing on the grounds of autonomy to take the required courses for the degree. My main point in this chapter has been that this is neither Kant's notion of autonomy nor a desirable notion of it.

There is, however, one way in which I have gone beyond Kant. The sense of call to me in applying to Calvin was particular. It was a call to *me* and my family, and not (as I experienced it) a call to anyone in my sort of situation to do that sort of thing. For Kant this already prevents my response from being moral, because it is not universal, and this also prevents it from being autonomous. Here I think Kant is wrong about God's moral prescriptions and about morality in general. Henry Stob is right to complain that Kant has misunderstood the role in morality of rational law. Stob is wrong, though, to say that Kant has put rational law on the *empty throne* from which he has excluded God. I hope I have demonstrated this in this chapter. I have tried to stress what I called the vertical dimension of Kant's moral thought. We can then put this Kantian notion of autonomous submission together with Scotus's view of our final end. We can be autonomous if we trust God to tell us to do what will in the end produce the highest intrinsic good, namely (as Scotus puts it) that we become co-lovers with God. So we carry out our obligations because God has made them obligatory, but also because we share this end with God.

We can go back one last time to Peter and Sue, the example in the introduction. Is Peter exercising his autonomy in choosing to return to Sue, or is he merely like a child obeying its parent? But hearing God's call in his situation and obeying it are no easy thing. It takes a mature attention and self-discipline, and the experience that there is in the end blessing from obedience, both for oneself and others. If Peter has known God's love before, he can trust that this time as well he will be given the resources he needs to do what seems (without God) impossible, and that in the end doing things God's way is best. But at the time of the choice what keeps him going is the sheer imperative to align himself with God, and this does not seem like abrogating but like exercising his freedom.

Let me try to sum up in a couple of sentences where we have got to over the three chapters of this book as a whole. I have tried to show that there is a structure in our evaluations which engages both the good outside us and our heart's response. I suggested that a theist can see this pull to the good as part of the created order, the pull of God towards being co-lovers. But when we make value judgments, we are not merely registering that pull but endorsing it or resisting it. Evaluation here expresses the fundamental orientation of our hearts. "Where your treasure is, there shall your heart be also." God's commands, I have said, can be seen as the route God has chosen for us to reach the destination of being co-lovers with God. This means that the character of the commands is not, in the end, merely dictatorial but relational — heading us towards union. But since morality is relational in this way, it has to be seen as involving also our autonomous submission to these commands. Because we share a final end with God, our submission is not blind, though we may not always see how the route leads to the end. But when we evaluate in a full-blooded way, our will is engaged either in endorsing the pull or in resisting it. This is how the objective and the subjective sides of evaluation are related. This is also how to understand God's authority in human morality.

INDEX